sevensacredpauses

Living Mindfully Through the Hours of the Day

"Time is money, and money is scarce." All who are driven by this double misconception get squeezed into a frantic rat race. Macrina Wiederkehr shows you a way out: the ancient art of returning again and again to the great Now that is beyond time. Speaking from experience—her own and that of centuries of Benedictine life—she can lead you out of the time trap into a joy no money can buy.

David Steindl-Rast, O.S.B.
Author of *The Music of Silence*

This terrific book brings the ancient prayer of the Church into modern focus as the author invites the readers to mark the moments of the day with prayer. She offers inspiration galore to feed the soul in simple, yet profound everyday—hourly—ways.

Religion Teacher's Journal

. . . [A] wonderful resource for those who routinely pray the hours, whether communally or privately. It offers an effective antidote to the monotony and distraction that can imperceptibly drain daily prayer of life and meaning. Reading this book, one will awaken to the deeper symbolic dimensions of each hour and thereby be able to redirect one's energy towards a fuller, faith-filled, cosmic participation.

Cistercian Studies Quarterly

This inspiring devotional resource will serve as a catalyst to spur your own practice of being present and paying attention to the sacred rhythms of the day.

Spirituality & Practice

A mini-retreat for the soul, this book will inspire, challenge, and delight its readers.

Spirit & Life

Seven Sacred Pauses is an invitation into the wisdom, archetypal images, and unique mood of each of the traditional seven hours. Each hour offers a unique and intimate conversation with God.

St. Placid Priory

sevensacredpauses

Living Mindfully Through the Hours of the Day

macrina wiederkehr
Author of *A Tree Full of Angels*

SORIN BOOKS Notre Dame, Indiana

Copyright acknowledgements

Every effort has been made to properly acknowledge all copyrighted material used in this book. The Publisher regrets any oversights and will correct any errors in future printings.

All prayers not attributed to an author are the work of Macrina Wiederkehr and are protected under the copyright of this work.

Unless otherwise noted, scripture quotations are from the New Revised Standard Version of the Bible, copyright © 1993 and 1989 by the Division of Christian Education of the National Council of Churches of Christ in the U.S.A. Used by permission. All rights reserved.

"The Heron," copyright © 1958 by John Ciardi from *I marry you; a sheaf of love Poems*. Used by permission of the Ciardi Family Trust.

"Rise Early" is from *Circle of Life*, copyright © 2005 by Joyce Rupp and Macrina Wiederkehr. Used by permission of Sorin Books, P.O. Box 428, Notre Dame, IN 46556. All rights reserved.

"Keeping Watch" is from *I Heard God Laughing*, by Hafiz, copyright © 1996 and 2002 by Daniel Ladinsky and used with his permission.

The chants by Velma Fry are reprinted with her permission from the CD, *Seven Sacred Pauses: Singing Mindfully Dawn Through Day*. All rights reserved.

"The Visit" is used by permission of Patricia Lunetta. All rights reserved.

"Incorrigible Exuberance Shared" is used by permission of Lee Self. All rights reserved.

"A thousand colors is your Face" originally appeared in *Seasons of Your Heart* as part of "A Vespers Sunset Prayer." Copyright © 1991 by Macrina Wiederkehr. Used by permission of HarperCollins Publishing. All rights reserved.

"Let Evening Come Upon Us" is used by permission of Judith Brower, O.S.B. All rights reserved.

"Love Made Visible" and "O Impermanence!" are used by permission of Beth Fritsch. All rights reserved.

"Illumination Please" and "The Old One" are used by permission of Karen Ewan. All rights reserved.

"Night Rain" is excerpted from *Weaving the Wind*, copyright © 2006 by Antoinette Voûte Roeder and used by permission of Apocryphile Press, Berkeley, CA.

www.sorinbooks.com

Hardcover ISBN-10 1-933495-10-3   ISBN-13 978-1-933495-10-1
Paperback ISBN-10 1-933495-24-3   ISBN-13 978-1-933495-24-8
eBook ISBN-10 1-933495-45-6   ISBN-13 978-1-933495-45-3

Cover and text design by John Carson.

Printed and bound in the United States of America.

Library of Congress Cataloging-in-Publication Data
Wiederkehr, Macrina.
  Seven sacred pauses : living mindfully through the hours of the day / Macrina Wiederkehr ; foreword by Paula D'Arcy.
    p. cm.
  Includes bibliographical references (pp. 195–203)
  ISBN-13: 978-1-933495-10-1
  ISBN-10: 1-933495-10-3
  1. Prayers. 2. Prayer books. 3. Meditations. 4. Divine office. 5. Devotional literature. I. Title.
  BV245.W483 2008
  242--dc22

                    2007048756

For Sister Norbert Hoelting, O.S.B.,
cherished mentor, woman of wisdom,
original inspiration for my monastic journey.

Contents

Gratitudes

"Gratitude is the heart's memory," an old proverb acknowledges. As this book comes to print, I am aware how true these words are. Here you will find a list of my heart's memories.

—Velma Frye, for her gift of music and her willingness to collaborate with me on these seven sacred pauses through the creation of a companion CD. My heart's memories include our retreat at Dog Island in Florida where we met for several days, along with Mary Beth McBride, to honor the hours through prayerful reflection.

—Ron and Tami Danielak, Paula D'Arcy, Mary Dowe, Julie Palmer, Rosann Vaughn, Rosanne Wood, the Sisters of the Cenacle Retreat House in Houston, and the Sisters of Hesychia House of Prayer in Arkansas, who provided me with the sacred space and solitude that is so essential for the creative process.

—My monastic community of St. Scholastica Monastery in Fort Smith, Arkansas, who lovingly tolerates my creative distractions and varying moods as we prayerfully move through the hours together. You are central to my heart's memories.

—My readers and retreatants who in so many ways continue to stir up my creative spirit as they encircle me with their support and encouragement.

—Kaye Bernard, Margaret Burns, Elise Forst, Karen Hahn, John King, Elaine Magruder, Jay McDaniel, Annabelle

Clinton Imber, Becky Oates, Heather Roques, Joyce Rupp, Magdalen Stanton, Christie Stephens, and Bernice Grabber Tintis, who read parts of my manuscript and offered me valuable suggestions, observations, and support.

—Sr. Ginger deGravelle, Sr. Mary Dennison, Karen Ewan, Beth Fritsch, Velma Frye, and Joanne Simsick, who have been exceptionally significant in the shaping of this book.

—And of course, my heart's memories include the wonderful people at Ave Maria and Sorin Books who have portrayed such enthusiasm during the process of creating *Seven Sacred Pauses*: for my editor Bob Hamma's dedication and guidance, publisher Tom Grady's openness to this project, publicist Keri Suarez and all those in marketing, especially Mary Andrews and Julie Cinninger. To all who work behind the scenes, I am grateful for you.

Meister Eckhart is on target when he says, "If the only prayer you ever say in your entire life is *thank you,* it will be enough." So that is my prayer. THANK YOU!

Foreword

I remember an evening I spent more than ten years ago. I had arrived a day early to lead a retreat at Laity Lodge, a retreat center set in the rocky, beautiful hill country of south-central Texas. Madeleine L'Engle had been staying there for a month, writing and intermittently speaking to retreat groups. She was leaving the next morning, but that evening she and I and our mutual friend, Betty Anne Cody, had planned to have dinner in Leakey, Texas, at a local café. (Think *very* local, think colorful, think beef or catfish, think delicious.) Driving back to the Lodge after dinner was a dark, steep descent into the heart of the Frio Canyon. The dirt roads had no shoulders and were challenging even in daylight because of the steep drop-offs. Betty Anne inched the car along slowly, pebbles spitting out from beneath the wheels, until she turned, at Madeleine's suggestion, into a lookout point where we sat for a long while beneath the breathtaking stars.

When we finally reached our rooms, Madeleine invited me to join her and Betty Anne as they prayed Compline (night prayer). Together we reviewed the day and read ancient words from the prayer book—words that have been intoned for centuries. This sweet, simple joining of three hearts, "remembering hours" together, has stayed as a strong, rich memory. Certainly it mattered because of the circle of friendship and the brilliant display of the heavens still bursting in our hearts. But more than that, as Macrina will teach you in this poetic and beautiful guide, the night prayers became a force of love that "embraced us as we entered the Great Silence of night." In the praying of the hours, in the very act of turning our intention to the Spirit filling the night, we aligned ourselves with the power in our midst.

Over the years I have often been a guest at Macrina's monastery. I've heard the ringing of the bell, calling the sisters to pray. I've felt the sweep of their shadows as they put down the work in front of them and moved silently to their seats in a dimly lit chapel. And I am always moved and confronted by the way they change their daily rhythm to conform to the movement of God. There (and in many monasteries) I've listened to stories, often told with great humor, about the sisters' first days in religious life . . . and the early struggle to adjust their active ways to the rhythm of the hours. But the ending of the story is always the birth of deep respect and devotion, born out of obedience to this simple call. Macrina writes, ". . . [in time] listening is transformed into prayer." I find hope for the world in her eloquent observation: "That by bringing ourselves continually back to remembrance of Spirit, we truly pray. We recommit. We believe that peace in the world is possible."

Today many monasteries are filled with lay women and men, as well as religious. We, too, move through those long monastery corridors as we make retreats and days of reflection. We don't live day by day according to a chosen Rule, as the sisters and monks do, but we are still searching for a way to faithfully become conscious of "the grace of each hour." Our hearts yearn.

In this beautiful handbook Macrina opens the monastery door. She invites us into a greater awareness of the monastic tradition and offers guidance for the journey. Here, she says, is the way to bring this practice home to your own heart. Here is how to live in the world and still remain faithful to the light and darkness. Here is how to summon the holy of your own divine self. She asks, Why not make this pilgrimage through the day with a heart for one another? Then she adds, If you want to learn—you practice.

Macrina's dear self is such a worthy guide. You are holding in your hands not only a book of readings and instruction for the journey, but one monastic's heart of love held out to a searching world.

Paula D'Arcy
Austin, Texas
January 28, 2007

Introduction

More and more people find
themselves drinking
at the wells of each other's
spiritual traditions,
and engaging in a deep and
common quest.
—Jim Wallis

These words have found a nesting place in my heart, and the beautiful truth they contain is like a prayer shawl that I keep wrapping around my great longing for spiritual communion with all beings.

I am steeped in the spirituality of Jesus, deeply rooted in Christianity. This is where my home is. I believe that when roots go deep enough, eventually they entangle with other roots. This entangling, it seems to me, ought to bring us joy, but often it fills us with fear. I want to give up my fear of other religious traditions. I want to wrap my prayer shawl around our entangled and entwined roots in the lovely gesture of a blessing so that we may continue our spiritual quest together and learn from each other's sacred practices.

As a member of a Benedictine community I have been blessed by the practice of honoring "the hours" through conscious pausing for prayer at specific times of the day. When

I speak of the hours I am referring to those times of the day that the earth's turning offers us: midnight, dawn, midmorning, noon, midafternoon, evening, and night. Although every hour is sacred, these special times have been hallowed by centuries of devotion and prayer.

Seven Sacred Pauses is a book of reflections based on the themes of the hours that monastics have remained faithful to through the ages. It is meant to be a guide for those who would like to move through their day with greater mindfulness. In particular, I have in mind those who do not live in monastic communities yet are searching for ways to be more attuned to the present moment. It is possible to develop a kindred spirit with these rich historical hours that does not require praying specific texts or going to a particular place for prayer. Each hour has its own unique mood and special grace. You can learn to enter into the spirit of the hour wherever you are. No matter what you are doing, you can pause to touch the grace of the hour.

Living in harmony with the hours requires faithful practice in the art of mindfulness. Surely the reason monastic orders of all religious traditions have adopted the practice of pausing at specific hours of the day is for the purpose of practicing mindfulness, yet when I lead retreats, inevitably someone will ask me about the word *mindfulness* with a tone of caution, suggesting that this is a Buddhist concept. It is true that Buddhists have long been faithful to the practice of mindfulness, but striving to live mindfully is a universal quest and belongs to us all. Living mindfully is the art of living awake and ready to embrace the gift of the present moment.

When I pray the gospels, it is crystal clear that Jesus had a rhythm of prayer in his life. He lived mindfully. We see him withdrawing from the apostles and from his crowds of followers. He takes time for solitude at critical moments in his life. He goes away at significant times of the day—dawn, for example. Sometimes he spends the whole night in prayer. He seeks out lonely places where he can be silent and in communion with God. Often he slips away at crucial times of strife or moments when decisions need to be made, yet he always returns to his ministry of compassion and love among the people.

After Jesus' death and resurrection we see his disciples attempting to honor the same inborn need to pause in prayerful remembrance at specific hours of the day. The Catholic monastic hours grew out of the spirit of the early Christian households of faith, which continued to meet in the temple for prayer and celebrate the breaking of bread in their homes (Acts 2:42–47). These hours have been revised and expanded in many ways and have, in the course of history, been known by various names: the canonical hours, the Divine Office, the Prayer of the Hours, the Divine Hours, the Liturgy of the Hours.

An old book by Pius Parsch, *The Breviary Explained,* became a vital resource for me as I began to reflect on the value of pausing for prayer throughout the day. I was taken by surprise at the beauty of the hours and the immeasurable wisdom of moving to the natural rhythm of the days and nights. The daily and nightly dance of the hours is a universal way of honoring the earth's turning as well as the sacred mysteries that flow out of our Christian heritage. This ancient tradition of inviting people to move through the day remembering their Source of Life is not a practice that has died. It is alive and well in many traditions.

Many people, even those who are not monastics, have tried to be faithful to these hours in a shortened form. The four-volume Liturgy of the Hours, a condensed version of the original monastic hours, has been an immense gift and support to many people who try to pray at least part of the hours of the day.

St. Benedict wanted his monks to pray through the entire psalter, all 150 psalms, in a week. In our modern world this is not feasible. The Prayer of the Hours has gone through many revisions, and the customs and traditions of various communities are not always the same. Although the intention of this book is to provide you with poetic reflection material on the *spirit* of the hours rather than the historical *text* of the hours, it seems important to give you a brief look at the historic hours that monastics have prayed throughout the ages. This will be especially helpful for those of you who are not familiar with the history of their use.

The Seven Sacred Pauses

"At midnight I rise to give you thanks . . ." we proclaim in Psalm 119:62, and in verse 164 of the same psalm we pray, "seven times a day I praise you. . . ." The early church and monastic communities have tried to honor the invitation of these scriptural texts in the following manner:

Matins or Vigils

Traditionally this hour was prayed in the heart of the night. However, due to the fragility of the human condition, it is understandable that in many communities Matins was moved to the early morning hours when it was still dark. It became a pre-dawn prayer. Even some parish churches honored the office of Matins. I recall my dad getting up in the wee hours of the morning on certain feast days to go to church for Matins. In some monasteries it is still the custom to pray Matins, more commonly called Vigils. The theme for this hour is vigilance. Those who keep vigil are sentinels of the night. I call this hour "The Night Watch."

Lauds or Morning Prayer

This early morning hour, ideally prayed at sunrise, is the first of the day hours and has praise and resurrection as its central themes. The dawn, too, has its sentinels. Rising early, they watch for the coming of the light. Perhaps on some mornings you can join the sentinels of dawn, as you, too, wait for the coming of the new light. I call this "The Awakening Hour."

Terce or the Third Hour of the Day

Terce, Sext, and None are referred to as the "little hours" because they are shorter and come right in the heart of the workday. They are simple efforts to turn our thoughts ever so briefly back to God, to the dance of life, to mindfulness of the present moment. Pius Parsch calls them *breathing spells for the soul,* a little oasis for one's spirit in the midst of work.

If we remember to pause at midmorning, we may experience a holy presence emanating from within. The blessing we seek is already in us. This brief pause opens the heart to receive the Spirit's gift. We invite the Spirit into our work as we pause to remember the noble nature of work. I call this "The Blessing Hour."

Sext or the Sixth Hour

This is the hour of light. The sun, having reached its peak in the heavens, illuminates all things. This is the hour of courage, recommitment, and passion. It is a good hour to practice believing that peace in the world is possible. I call this "The Hour of Illumination."

None or the Ninth Hour

As day moves toward evening with wisdom in its wings, this is the hour to reflect on impermanence, aging, death, and transition. The dance steps may be slower, but there is also a keen insightfulness in those steps, along with a wise knowing of what is most important in life. I call this "The Wisdom Hour."

Vespers or Evensong

In this twilight hour it is time to move from the tumult
of the day into the quiet of evening. However, due to the
busy lifestyle of most modern-day people, finding their own
Vespers path will be necessary. Vespers is the hour that is most
often prayed festively and publicly; thus you may want, on
occasion, to search out a monastery, church, or some other
praying community with which to celebrate this beautiful
hour. I call this "The Twilight Hour."

Compline or Night Prayer

This is the last hour of the day and is often prayed privately or in small groups. In this night hour we are a bit more
subjective, turning our thoughts inward. It is time to review
your day by means of a gentle evaluation of your faithfulness
as a pilgrim of the hours. Trust in God and personal sorrow
for failures are partners in this last dance in the seasons of the
day. This is the hour of intimacy. It is love rather than guilt
that ought to enrobe us as we enter what monastics call "The
Great Silence" of night.

These hours are important archetypal images of the
rhythm and movement of the day. The wisdom of pausing
at these sacred times is a treasure that ought not be lost. For
this reason I am offering you a way of continuing the ancient
dance of the hours. Hopefully you will be drawn to make
these seven sacred pauses a part of your daily practice. Using

scripture, poetic prose, poetry, song, personal stories, and quotes from other seekers, I have tried to capture the spirit of each hour. May you be able to respond in a way that is authentic for you on your unique spiritual path.

What I Have Learned from the Hours

For many years I have prayed the Divine Office with my monastic community. One of the things I have learned is the importance of the bell. The bell calls us to the Prayer of the Hours. The bell is annoying. The bell is good. I have learned to change the annoying sound of the bell into an instrument of invitation. Just as the sun will not wait to rise if I am not there for the occasion, so too the community will not wait to pray if I am not there. What if God should choose to speak to the community and I wasn't present? What if the words I most needed to hear at this hour were, "Waste no energy fretting . . . " (Ps 37:7)? What if I wasn't there to receive them? The hours do not wait for me; they move on into eternity without me. I have learned that I truly want to be there—awake and mindful of the grace of each hour.

I have learned that no matter how much I want to be soulfully present at the Prayer of the Hours, the mind has a way of wandering. It can go back to the work I thought I had laid aside. The only way I know of dealing with this meandering creature is to faithfully practice bringing it back home to my heart.

I have learned in accepting the *new* never to totally discard the *old*. Although I have moved through many revised books of the Prayer of the Hours, I have always kept the book of hours we were using when I entered the monastery in the late fifties close at hand. We were the first monastic community in the United States to change from Latin to English. That little monastic breviary containing Latin on one side of the page and English on the other is the book that goes with me on most of my travels. It is a good memory and a dear contact with the past.

From the hymns in that old book of hours I have learned that our early Christian ancestors were very much in harmony with the sacredness of the changing seasons and the symbols of light and darkness. They were surprisingly creation-centered, considering how long ago that prayer book was compiled. Reference was often made to the light of the new day that the circling earth offers us each morning. To give you a sample of this faithful presence to the light and darkness, a verse from Monday morning Lauds reads:

> Glide in, thou very Sun divine;
> With everlasting brightness shine:
> And shed abroad on every sense
> The Spirit's light and influence.

And from Friday morning Lauds,

> The day-star's rays are glittering clear,
> And tell that day itself is near:
> The shadows of the night depart;
> Thou holy Light, illume the heart.

I have learned to be attentive to what speaks to the deepest ground of my being. When I was a young sister, one of my favorite parts of the Office was reflecting on the antiphons

that we prayed before and after the psalms. Antiphons are
tiny prayers usually drawn from scripture. For example:
"Hide me in the shadow of your wings" (Ps 17:8), or "O Lord
my God, in you I take refuge" (Ps 7:1). The shortness of the
antiphons makes them good material for meditation. When I
am praying with the community, I often find myself gleaning
from the psalms a few words to take with me into the day or
the night. During Vespers recently, I chose from Psalm 25,
"Release my trapped heart." Those few words became my
week's companion.

In my past experience of praying the hours in community,
I now realize that we sometimes sacrificed quality prayer by
putting too much emphasis on quantity. I am referring to the
duty of "getting all the prayers in." There were times when
we had to attend meetings or other events and could not be
at community prayer. At times such as these it would surely
have been wiser to pray one psalm slowly and with reverence
rather than hurrying through all the psalms and readings
assigned to that hour.

I recall religious of other communities sharing stories
about praying two or three of the hours in one prayer period,
just to fit in all the required prayers for the day. Listening to
these stories with my mind wide open to the value and beauty
of the Liturgy of the Hours, I believe one of the important
elements we missed in the past was developing an attitude
of mindfulness—a heart open to the spirit of the hour. The
spirit lives in the space between the words. The danger in
becoming too wordy is that we miss the space between the
words.

Today I have learned to be more flexible. When I cannot be with my community, I pray alone, often trying to pray at the same hour they are praying. At these times I ordinarily choose fewer psalms and pray the Office more contemplatively with longer pauses for reflection.

Perhaps most of all, I have learned that way down underneath all the busyness, something (or is it Someone?) waits for us to come home to who we truly are. All it takes is a simple pause to get us in touch with the One who keeps vigil with us—the holy presence of so many names. Only you can name that which waits for you.

Perhaps it is your true self. Or, maybe it is one of the virtues wanting to make its full presence known in your life. It may be the Divine Beloved. Remember to pause so that you may be able to connect to that which keeps vigil in your heart.

The dream of creating a meditation book centered on the spirit of the hours has been stirring in me for a long time. Instead of dying, this dream continued to grow—thus, the creation of *Seven Sacred Pauses*. I would like for this book to help ease the violence many of us carry in our hearts due to a stressful, multitasking work environment. I hope it will offer you a practice that can assist you in living with greater attention and intention. I hope you will remember to pause.

The Importance of Honoring the Hours

For Judaism, Christianity, and Islam—all Abrahamic religions—bells, chimes, or tonal sounds are important for calling people to prayer. For all these religions, the call to prayer is announced at specific hours. Special hours of the day are honored. For Islam the five daily rituals of prayer (*salat*) are pre-dawn, noon, afternoon, sunset, and night. The three times of gathering for prayer in Judaism are morning, afternoon, and night. In the Jewish tradition the oldest fixed daily prayer is the beautiful *Shema:*

> Hear, O Israel, the Lord Our God is one. Therefore you shall love the Lord, your God, with all your heart, and with all your soul, and with all your strength. (Deut. 6:4-5)

The Shema, an assertion of faith in One God, is recited when rising in the morning and upon retiring at night. It is the first prayer a Jewish child is taught, the last words spoken prior to death. The faithful recitation of the Shema brings about an experiential awareness of the Eternal One.

When the early Christians began to detach themselves from Judaism, they kept the practice of praying at fixed times of the day. As monastic communities began to form, other hours of the day were eventually added to the monastic day.

Indigenous peoples of varied ethnic groups have honored creation's mysterious and sacred rhythms of the seasons of the day and night for ages upon ages. There is something in the cycles of the earth that speaks to the restless human heart. When we truly listen to the call of the seasons of the day and the year, our listening is transformed into what many people call prayer.

It is my hope that people of diverse religious traditions, as well as people with no religious persuasion, will feel at home with this book. The division in our churches over what we call "religion" is heart-rending. I am deeply concerned about the increasing violence and fear in our world. The prayer of honoring the hours might be common ground for us. No matter what faith tradition we follow, we are pilgrims together on each day's journey. We all have to get up in the morning and move through the day with as much grace as we can gather. Why not make this pilgrimage through the day with a heart for one another, pausing throughout the day whether this be for two, five, or ten minutes? If we do this, someone will be pausing at every minute of the day. There will always be someone who is summoning the holy, practicing silence, standing still for remembrance of God. Our own divine selves—so prone to being smothered and forgotten in the many tasks of the day—will be acknowledged and reverenced.

Honoring the hours through seven sacred pauses has the potential of unfolding as a spiritual practice for many faith traditions. I believe that the word *practice* is one of the most important words in the spiritual life. If you want to be a dancer, a pianist, a singer, a figure skater, you practice. If you want to make the team in any area of sports, you practice. Just imagine the many hours of practice given over to those who make it to the Olympics. Why should the spiritual life be any different? We practice pausing to remember the sacredness of our names, who we are, and what we plan on doing with the incredible gift of our lives—and how we can learn to *be* in the midst of so much *doing*. We have to practice loving and forgiving. We practice breathing and being careful with one another's life. We practice nonviolence. We practice enjoying what we have rather than storing up possessions. We practice silence.

In one of his poems, the German poet Rainer Maria Rilke is talking to the "Great Mystery" that has haunted him throughout his life. He uses the image of "God's hands cupped around our becoming." With gentle eloquence the poet has God asking us to live, to die, and to be.

Seven Sacred Pauses highlights your call to *be*. Seven times during the day you are invited to reflect on the wondrous gift of being. Divine hands are still cupped around your becoming, and the best way to cooperate with those hands is to practice *being* present.

Our *being* is often crowded out by our *doing*. Each day we are summoned to be creators of the present moment. Artists know the value of white space. Sometimes what isn't there enables us to see what is. Perhaps you are being called to the spiritual practice of bringing a little of the white space—of *nada*—into your workday. There in that white space you will find your soul waiting for you. Allow the anointing rhythm of the hours to touch and teach you each day.

Suggestions for Using This Book

In these meditations on *the hours* I have created a pilgrim path for you. My primary intent is to offer you some contemplative moments in the midst of your day. The sacred pauses are seven invitations to mindfulness. Even those of you who pray all or part of the Liturgy of the Hours, alone or in community, may find this a valuable resource. If you use these

meditations for daily reflection, you may be surprised at how blessings unfold in your life. This is not a guide book on how to pray the Liturgy of the Hours. It is a rhythmical path of life that you can choose to walk each day. My suggestion is for you to use these poetic reflections for spiritual reading. Learn to live with the spirit of the hours in your heart. Take the themes into your memory. The medicine of deep listening taken seven times a day can be a healing companion in your workplace. Dream of a different way of approaching your work each day.

Understandably, you may not be able to consciously pray the seven hours every day. One way to approach these hours would be to make a cognizant choice about which hour you will focus on each day. Look at your schedule and decide which of the hours you might be able to fit into your agenda on any given day. This would be a time for you to intentionally pause from your work and remember the spirit of the hour.

At the end of each hour are some suggested prayers, poems, psalms, and antiphons for you to use as is helpful and according to your day's schedule. Let your creativity guide you. This book holds a variety of ways to assist you in living more mindfully each day. Live in a way that is kind to your soul. Keep vigil with your life.

A special CD, *Seven Sacred Pauses: Singing Mindfully Dawn Through Dark,* has been created by Velma Frye as a companion to this book (www.velmafrye.com). Some of these chants are traditional and may be familiar to you. Others have been created by Velma, gleaned from writings in this book or of her own creation. You may wish to let one of the

assigned chants fill your soul with music during your pause. If it is a chant you have memorized, the melody and words will quite easily echo through your being, drawing you into the present moment. The lyrics for the chants are found in a special section at the end of the book.

Another very fine resource for praying the hours can be found by going to Br. David Steindl-Rast's Web site (www. gratefulness.org) and clicking on the "Angel of the Hour." A prayer for each hour will be waiting for you along with a moving Gregorian chant.

These meditations on the hours are ideal for a personal retreat. Consider taking a day for reflection two or three times a year. Go to a retreat center, a cabin in the woods, or a lake. Practice living the hours with greater awareness. Be a conscious pilgrim of the hours for one day. A day of solitude is almost always valuable in bringing you back to your work with a renewed heart.

O Pilgrim of the Hours

Each morning
night's curtain
opens on a new day.
You are invited
to join the great opening.
Open your ears.
Open your heart.

Open your eyes
to the sacred path
you travel every day,
the path of the hours.

Greet the hours
with joyful awareness.
Greet the hours
with faithful presence.
Greet the hours
with a reverential bow.
Greet the hours
with a sacred pause.

Reverence each hour
as a small stepping stone
on your pilgrimage
through the day.
Receive the gift
of seven sacred pauses.
Practice waking up
seven times a day.

—Macrina Wiederkehr

Living Mindfully

The mysticism of everyday life
is the deepest mysticism of all.
                                    —Jürgen Moltmann

There are times when ordinary experiences that have been part of our lives day after day suddenly speak to us with such a radiant force it seems as though they are miracles. In his spiritual autobiography *The Golden String*, Bede Griffiths describes an evening walk when he was taken by surprise in a way that had never happened to him before. This experience significantly changed his life, drawing him into a more mindful way of living. As he walked alone at dusk, the birds were singing in full chorus, the hawthorne trees were bursting with bloom, the fading sun was casting color across the fields. As everything grew still and the veil of darkness began to cover the earth, he paints a picture of his feelings with these words:

> I remember now the feeling of awe which came
> over me. I felt inclined to kneel on the ground, as
> though I had been standing in the presence of an
> angel; and I hardly dared to look on the face of the
> sky, because it seemed as though it was but a veil
> before the face of God.

Listening to the description of this ordinary yet mystical experience, I can hear my friend Paula D'Arcy saying, "Everything in the universe breathes for God. It does not matter what name is given to this Presence." The truth of her words resonate deep in the ground of my being.

The mystical possibilities of every moment are revealed to us in our intentional pauses. There are, of course, times when we are startled into pausing because grace takes hold of us in an unexpectedly profound manner as it did for Bede Griffith on his evening walk. Suddenly we see the aura, the holy light, exuding from all things. More often, though, we need to practice living in such a way that our pauses become treasured anointings in the midst of our work. If we practice living mindfully, we slowly begin to see the holiness of so many things that remain hidden when we choose to rush through the hours, striking tasks from the list of things we must accomplish before day's end. It will be a happy moment when we remember to add the wise act of pausing to our to-do lists.

This pause can be as simple as standing attentively before a flowering plant or listening to the frogs in the pond. Perhaps we can stop for a cleansing breath: Breathe in the spirit of the hour; breathe in gratitude and compassion for yourself; breathe out love and encouragement for your coworkers, friends, family members. Your pause may be an awakening stretch, or sitting quietly and remembering your name. If you can learn the art of pausing, your work will prosper and be blessed. Ask yourself: Is it possible to be less busy and still productive? Is it possible to look at work as a ministry rather than just a means of employment? Or, could it be that in order to bring my best self into my workspace, I need to change my attitude about my work? Perhaps the answer to these questions depends on how efficient we can become in remembering to take breathing spells at these special hours of the day. Can we remember to pause? Throughout the hours of the day, whenever you feel stressed and overwhelmed, instead of pushing yourself to work harder and faster, remember to pause.

As a monastic in our modern world I, too, struggle with the need to help make a living for my community; yet implanted in the monastic heart is the desire to learn how to make a life rather than just a living. We are to seek God in all situations. The busyness that is so much a part of our lives can take its toll on us if we do not learn how to balance work, prayer, and leisure. The practice of pausing throughout the day in order to get in touch with the soul has deep roots in monastic life. It is not easy to step aside from our work, take a cleansing breath, and ask ourselves soul questions. Most of us don't like to disrupt our agenda. We often have schedules that seem set in stone. Pausing may seem like an unnecessary interruption, serving only to get us off schedule.

Breathing Spells for the Soul

You may have heard the story about some westerners who hired a few bushmen guides to help them travel through the Kalahari Desert. Not being used to moving at the pace their employers were expecting, the bushmen suddenly sat down to rest, and no amount of persuasion could induce them to continue the journey until they were ready. The reason for this much needed rest, the bushmen explained, was that they had to wait for their souls to catch up. Stories come to us when we need them, and it is my hunch that this is a story we need today. Indigenous peoples often have an innate awareness of the need to honor the natural pace and rhythm of their inner beings. They seem able to pick up signals drawing them into a stance of obedient listening. The bushman of the Kalahari called this ancient knowing "the tapping of the heart."

Many of us can relate to this story. We, too, can remember moments when we have heard the tapping of the heart. Listening to that deep inner voice of the soul and honoring the call to take care of ourselves can become a way of life. Most of us are in desperate need of breathing spells for the soul. Our days are frenetic—filled with activity. Although some of this activity is nourishing and replenishing, much of it is draining and numbing. All of this takes a toll on the soul. Our conversations often center around how busy we are, and phrases such as "I don't have time" become a frequent part of our dialogue. We find ourselves multitasking just to get through the day with some sense of accomplishment.

In regard to all this busyness in our lives, however, I would like to offer an encouraging word. Since most of us are actually busy doing good things, could it be that how we approach our work is the issue rather than how much we have to do? If we do not have healthy work patterns, then the tendency when someone tries to get us out of our workaholic mode is to look busy, talk about our busyness, and recite the mantra, "I don't have time."

All too often in today's corporate world the workaholic is revered and esteemed. Some employees wanting to climb the corporate ladder vie with coworkers to see who can come in first and/or leave the office last. The game is a ruse, stealing personal time away from the individual. Unfortunately, a heart attack is often the wake-up call to slow down and re-evaluate what is essential in life.

How can we learn to open our hearts to simple grace-filled experiences, such as the one Bede Griffiths spoke of above? How can we become more aware of the yearning in our hearts for the healing balm of solitude? You don't have to be a monastic to experience these grace-filled moments. These moments are available every day. They are offered to the workaholic just as frequently as to the mindful person. It is all a matter of living with open eyes and sometimes a rearrangement of our values.

We belong to this earth, and the work we do is ultimately for the purpose of making our world a better place in which to live. When we begin our day, most of us probably do not approach our work with the awareness and belief that we are artists involved in continuing the work of creation. From the most sublime to the most menial, work is creativity. If we could truly believe this, many things might change in our workplaces and in our world at large. It is not necessarily our work that is the problem; perhaps it is our inability to be a loving companion to our work.

The Lebanese-American poet Kahlil Gibran suggests that our work is our love made visible. The way we approach our work is vital to our happiness and the good we are going to be able to do as artists and co-creators with God. The attitude with which we approach our work determines whether or not our work will become a love made visible.

The Sacredness of Work

The Benedictine tradition has always tried to honor the sacredness of work. Work is a service for the benefit of the entire world. It is easy for us to lose sight of this truth. The competition and aggressiveness of the workplace can make it difficult for us to find the sacred aspect of work. Workplaces can become brutal machines squeezing every ounce of mindful reflection out of our systems. Yet from the simplest forms of labor to the most sublime, all work is for the purpose of improving the quality of life. Our work enables us to bring grace and beauty to our world. For this reason we need to learn how to work from the heart. From whom must we seek permission to work mindfully, heartfully, soulfully? This is a subtle question. The permission we need may be from our very own selves.

Even monastics are in danger of losing vision of the sacredness of work. It is difficult for individuals to understand that there is a deeper purpose behind every assigned task, a purpose that goes far beyond just completing the job. When I wash dishes in our community, I try to be purposefully conscious of the fact that I am not washing dishes just to get them done. Getting finished ought not be my goal because, you see, if this is the case, then I miss the experience of washing the dishes. This is all part of living mindfully.

In *The Way of Chang Tzu*, edited and compiled by Thomas Merton, a marvelous story is told via the poem "The Woodcarver." In this poem a master woodcarver is commissioned to carve a bell stand for the high court. Upon viewing the completion of the woodcarver's exquisite piece of art, the prince of Lu wants to understand the secret of this marvelous masterpiece.

With beautiful simplicity and humility, the artist claims there is no secret. When he received this assignment, he put his entire being into the work, guarding his spirit from any sort of trivia that would take his mind away from the task at hand. He fasted so as to have a pure and single heart to bring to the work. In his mind's eye he constantly beheld the perfect bell stand holding the bell that would call people to work or to prayer.

In claiming that there was no special secret, the woodcarver was suggesting that the perfection of the bell stand was due to the loving dedication and undivided attention given to the task. We all have the potential to give ourselves wholeheartedly to whatever it is we must do. This is the gift of mindfulness. Each of us can learn to guard our hearts from trivia as we watch the work of our hands become a blessing.

The fact that the woodcarver was carving a bell stand is particularly significant for our meditation on the hours. Throughout the ages bells have been used to call peoples of all religious beliefs to significant tasks, especially to the work of prayer. When the bell peals out its melodious music, something awakens in us—the reverberation connects us to an ancient longing. It is a longing to be united to the Holy Source from which all things have emerged.

With practice we can learn to live as vessels of devotion, containers out of which we pour forth loving service to others. When I hear the bell, I pray for the grace to put aside the work I am doing. In listening to the bell I am actually listening to an invitation for union with the Beloved. In answering the bell I am proclaiming by my actions that there is an even greater Love than the loving service I am performing.

Living mindfully is not an option for those who want to live healthy lives. Healthy living necessitates finding a balance between work, prayer, and leisure. Integration of these three is difficult but not impossible. Daily practice is needed as well as, perhaps, waking up to our own inner call. A bell will not necessarily peal out for you in your workplaces. You must learn to listen for the tapping of the heart. In some workplaces this will be easier than others.

Corporate America will probably not bless you for taking care of yourself. The bottom line is production. Without that, there is no company. No one really cares what you did for them yesterday. The big question is: What are you going to do for me today? Thus the mania begins. It perpetuates itself, producing a stressed, violent society. It is impossible to be mindful when you are going ninety miles per hour.

Even if you aren't part of the big corporate machine, living mindfully is always a challenge. No matter what your work entails—housework, laundry, personal contacts, business meetings, preparing for workshops, yardwork, writing, composing, teaching, cooking, raising children, (fill in your own labor of love)—realize that you are an artist. In some small way you are continuing the work of creation. Remember to pause.

one

the night watch

Themes for the hour:
vigilance and deep listening
mystery and silence
surrender and trust

Midnight Until Dawn

Rising from sleep in the heart of the night, I keep vigil with eternal questions. These eternal questions are infinite longings that have taken root in the ground of my being. Holding vigil with the Guardian of Life, whose eye shines down upon all who live in terror of the night, I become quiet. In the middle of the night I hold hands with trust and surrender to the One who sees without a light. I, too, see without a light. I welcome my night eyes. My soul is my night light. Night vigil is a time for deep listening. My prayer travels deep into my soul space, into the essence of my being. I go "down under" where the eternal One waits. I wait with the One who waits for me. Like Jesus, keeping watch the night before he died, I keep vigil with those who wait alone. The darkness has a special kind of soul. I lean into the darkness and grow wise.

I rise before dawn and cry for help;
I put my hope in your words.
My eyes are awake before each watch of
the night,
that I may meditate on your promise.
—Psalm 119:147–148

During two transitional seasons in my spiritual life, I had the joy of being able to make a retreat at Gethsemane Abbey in Trappist, Kentucky. The deep silence I experienced was good medicine for me. It was a time in my life when "wordless words" were the only words I trusted; thus the silence was healing. It was a season of deep listening in my life.

During my retreats at Gethsemane I chose to attend Vigils with the monks. Getting up in the middle of the night can be a moving experience in the course of a retreat. The night watches cut into my soul with a terrible sweetness. I am certain beyond doubt that if I had to get up every night at two or three in the morning the sweetness would soon wear off. I suspect this is also true for the monks. Thus upon leaving the retreat and returning home, the gift I carried with me was the memory of the faithfulness of these monks rising to pray in the middle of the night. This monastery has become famous because it was the monastery of Thomas Merton. However, as I left the monastery, it was not Thomas Merton I was enamored of; it was remembrance of those present-day monks and their faithful night watch.

Although the practice of rising for prayer in the middle of the night is not observed in my community, there are times when I choose to rise for the night watch. These are usually times of national disaster or community crisis, although I am also fond of rising on the vigils of major feasts of the saints and Christ, and on the vigil of my birth.

At these special times when I rise from my sleep for prayer, I keep vigil with Christ, who is always keeping vigil. I keep vigil with my heart's eternal questions and deep longings and with those places in my being where the light has grown dim. I keep vigil with those whose tired hearts have lost hope. The angel of night embraces my prayer and lights a candle in my soul. Keeping watch at my side, she listens to my dreams for the world and my prayers for all who suffer. In the middle of night I pray for those who sleep and those who cannot sleep. I pray for those with fearful hearts, for those whose courage is waning. I pray for those who have lost vision of what could be. When I rise in the middle of the night, my prayer is simply one of waiting in silence, waiting in darkness, listening with love. It is a prayer of surrender. In my night watch I do not ordinarily use words. My prayer is a prayer of intent. I make my intention and I wait. I become a deep yearning. The silence and the darkness are healing. My prayer is now a prayer of trust. I keep vigil with the mystery.

There is something lovely about the darkness. When I say the angel of night lights a candle in my soul, I am not talking about the kind of candle that takes the darkness away. Rather, in the darkness and in the great silence I discover that my soul has an eye that can see in the dark and an ear that can hear in the silence. With my soul's eye, what needs to be seen is revealed in a new way; with my soul's ear, what needs to be heard is felt in a new way. It is a way of seeing with the heart and of listening from the soul, a way of understanding.

We know there are stars so far away that their light has not yet reached the earth. Could the same be said about the bright ideas, virtues, creativity, and dreams of our own lives? Perhaps some night when you get up to pray, something will turn over in someone's heart and find its voice all because of your small prayer. Never underestimate what little acts of love can accomplish. Do not take lightly the sacred connections that are possible in daily life. Perhaps our very waiting in the darkness gives some struggling unknown pilgrim of the hours hope.

In view of the fact that this meditation book is written with those of you who are in the workaday world in mind, you may wonder why I have included Vigils as one of your sacred hours of prayer. It is highly unlikely that you will be able to rise in the middle of the night for prayer. Many of you have families with children of various ages and activities, as well as demanding jobs already requiring more time than you can find.

Still, I see Vigils as a valuable part of this book. Vigils is a time of exquisite beauty. It is a time for waiting and watching under the mantle of mystery. It can be a prayer of waiting without agenda, without urgency. We often wait for things we cannot change. Waiting in itself has the potential of being a prayer of faith. Sometimes we wait for growth. Like a seed resting in the ground, we wait for who we can become. The darkness that surrounds us can be an ointment for our restless spirit. If we do not turn away from this darkness, it has the potential of becoming a nurturing womb for us. Often it is in the dark times of our lives that our eyes are opened, and we see things in new ways.

More than likely, there are times in your life when you celebrate Vigils without realizing you are praying. Search your life for moments of prayerful waiting and watching. Name some of your special hours of vigilance. Some of these moments may have come in the middle of the night, others may have been during the day. Keeping vigil is a natural part of our lives.

Do you recall times when you sat up with a sick child? That is a vigil. Karen, who often comes to our retreat center at St. Scholastica for quiet time, describes how her colicky baby led her into mysticism: "To quiet the cries, we would walk up and down our long driveway in the middle of the night, sometimes for over an hour, until comfort and sleep would come. The silence of our sojourn led me into a sacred union—with my son, the Divine, and the suffering of the whole world. In these treasured moments I felt connected to all of creation. I began to call this 'Colic Mysticism.'" Karen's experience is a good example of keeping vigil.

Have you waited for teenage children to come home safely at night? That, too, is a vigil. Or perhaps there have been times when you were awakened in the middle of the night for seemingly no reason at all. Perhaps you have lain awake with anxiety and worry. Maybe you have quarreled with a loved one and you cannot sleep out of concern over how to be reconciled. All of these moments and more can become natural vigils. These painful experiences can be transformed into creative waiting. You can rise out of your sleep or non-sleep at these moments, curl up in a favorite old chair, and keep vigil with your anxious heart.

We wait for the diagnosis after a series of medical tests, whether for ourselves or for a family member or friend. We wait for news after the surgery of a loved one. We wait for our children, and sometimes for our parents, to come home from war. We wait to hear if we got the job we applied for, or if our test scores will make it possible for us to attend the university of our choice. We wait for reconciliation and forgiveness. We wait for death.

Most of us do not like to wait. There is anxiety in waiting—whether we are waiting in a supermarket line, in the doctor's office, the I.R.S. office, at the bank, in a restaurant, at the stoplight, or any of the hundreds of places we have to wait each week. Waiting is not high on our list of priorities.

Not all vigils are anxiety-ridden. There is the joyful waiting for someone dear to come for a visit, or the waiting for an important event such as a marriage or the birth of a child. We wait for the seasons to come round again, for gardens to grow and flowers to bloom. Just as the gardener keeps vigil with the seed in the ground we, too, if we are alert to the goodness of spiritual waiting, can keep vigil with the seed that wants to sprout in our lives. We wait for who we will become.

There is a difference between waiting and keeping vigil. Anxious, fretful, impatient waiting is nothing more than waiting. Waiting with purpose, patience, hope, and love is *vigilant* waiting. Would that all of our waiting could be a vigil—a watch in the night or in the day hours. So by all means, find a way to make your vigils sacred. Learn the art of holy waiting. Whether you choose, on occasion, to get up in the middle of the night, or whether you make an effort to turn your everyday moments of waiting into sacred vigils rather than impatient pacing, you will be blessed through this spiritual practice.

In ancient times vigils were often connected with keeping watch on the eve of a great feast. The antiphons and prayers for the night vigil centered around the approaching feast. I love feasts because they suggest that there is always something in the midst of ordinary life to celebrate. We celebrate moments and memories of the lives of saints, of the heroes and heroines of our lives. We can also celebrate moments of our personal life journeys. There are milestones along the way: births and deaths, weddings, and anniversaries. Look for ways to keep vigil with these memorable events. Learn to create your own feast days. Every birthday is a little feast. I know a person who keeps vigil on the eve of her birth. With candle lit she waits in the darkness, keeping company with the miracle of her birth—that bittersweet journey from the darkness of the womb into a land of light.

In her book *A Candle at Midnight*, Marcy Heidish writes perceptively about the power of personal vigils. "Whether your vigil-keeping is centered around chronic illness, depression, personal crisis, national disaster, or simply the heart's yearning for a deepening relationship with God, self, and others, vigilance is a spiritual discipline and a special kind of prayer."

May you learn to live with a vigilant heart.

Prayers, Poetry, and Antiphons to Help You Celebrate the Night Watch

A Prayer Guide

Opening

My soul yearns for you, O God.
• I keep vigil with you through the night.

Sacred Song

In this sacred darkness I sit in silence.
Open in this moment, I trust in the darkness.
Waiting in trust, growing in trust.
Waiting and trusting the sacred darkness.
I surrender.

I surrender.
I surrender.

—Macrina Wiederkehr

(This song can be found on the CD *Seven Sacred Pauses: Singing Mindfully Dawn Through Dark.*)

Contemporary Psalm

Antiphon: My eyes are awake before each watch of the night, that I may meditate on your promise. (Psalm 119:148)

O Sentinel of the night skies,
Attendant of my soul's deep yearning.
Drawn into the night silence,
I keep vigil with eternal questions.

All through the night watch
I seek you without words.
Listening to the sound of silence,
I lean into the song of darkness
with infinite patience I wait for you.

Keeping vigil with eternal questions,
I do not look for answers; it is enough
to wait in the darkness of love's yearning.
My soul is my night light; I am not afraid.

Repeat Antiphon.

Biblical Psalm Suggestions for the Night Watch

Psalm 42
Psalm 63
Psalm 119:145–152

Closing Prayer

Select the Prayer of the Hour below or another prayer in this section.

Prayer of the Hour

O Love Divine and Mysterious . . .

Take me down deep to the holy darkness of Love's roots. Let me become one with the One I love. Draw me into the depths. Night prayer is deep prayer. Let me go deep. Teach me the art of waiting with patience that I may grow strong, loving, and wise.

Let me borrow your eyes O Beloved. Then I shall see in the dark.

Additional Prayers and Poems for the Night Watch

O Vigilant One . . .

You stand alert at the gate of our hearts. Tutor us in the fine art of keeping vigil that we may lovingly watch over the family of the earth with your own eyes of compassionate awareness. With you as our guide, perhaps our loving vigilance will enable us to become healers in a world of violence. Be present in the lives of those whose darkness is not a holy darkness. Be with those who never get to experience the therapeutic healing of the Great Silence. We surrender our own plans and enter your great plan for peace upon the earth. Give us attentive, peaceful hearts as we watch with you through the long dark night. We Bless You O Sacred Darkness.

O Guardian of our Lives . . .

Through our joys and our sorrows, you keep watch. Through our days and our nights, you keep watch. Through the passing of our years, you keep watch. In our youth and our aging, you keep watch. In our destruction of the earth, you keep watch. In our caring for the earth, you keep watch. In the midst of the violence on our earth, you keep watch. In our peaceful times, you keep watch. In the seasons of our hearts, you keep watch. Through the seasons of the years, you keep watch. Teach us, like you, to keep watch. Give us vigilant hearts.

Night Meditation to Help You Sleep

In the age in which we are living it is more than likely that there will be those among you who will be retiring when the monks are rising for the night vigil. Your body and mind have toiled throughout the day and need the gift of rest. If you are just retiring at the time of the night vigil, let the moment of lying down to rest be a prayer as you wait to fall asleep. The psalmist prays, "As soon as I lie down I fall peacefully asleep" (Ps 4:9). Even if this may not always be true in your case, it is a good prayer to close your day. Use it as an antiphon of trust, and let sleep become a prayer carrying you to a new world of dreams and hopes attained.

The Angel of Night

> Summoned from sleep
> in the heart of night
> my name is called
> and, like Samuel,
> I rise from my bed
> seeking the caller.
>
> Summoned from sleep
> I am drawn into
> the beating heart
> of the One
> who called me.

The angel of night
lights a candle in my soul
inviting me to listen
to the wordless song
of Divine Union.

Deep healing.
Deep listening.
Deep waiting.
Deep watching.
All of these become
a part of my night watch.

In the heart of the night
you prepare me to be
your deep healing
for all who watch
through the night
of their fears.

—Macrina Wiederkehr

Antiphons for the Night Watch

I rise before dawn and cry for help; I put my hope in your words.

—Psalm 119:147

My eyes are awake before each watch of the night that I may meditate on your promise.

—Psalm 119:148

A light to you in the darkness; a light when all other lights go out.

—J.R.R. Tolkien

Those who wait for the Lord shall renew their strength, they shall mount up with wings like eagles, they shall run and not be weary, they shall walk and not faint.

—Isaiah 40:31

And I said to the one who stood at the gate of the year, "Give me a light that I may tread safely into the Unknown." And he replied, "Go out into the darkness and put your hand into the hand of God. That shall be to you better than light and safer than a known way."

—Minnie Haskins

I have seen too many stars to let the darkness overwhelm me.

—Macrina Wiederkehr

. . . that which sings and contemplates in you is still dwelling within the bounds of that first moment which scattered the stars into space.

—Kahlil Gibran

Prayer goes deep at night. Images dissolve. There's only God, and silence, kindness, and grace.

—Coleman Barks

The darker the night, the lovelier the dawn she carries in her womb.

—Dom Helder Camara

One may not reach the dawn save by the path of the night.

—Germaine Greer

What in me is dark, illumine.

—John Milton

You will be very poor all the while you don't discover: It's not with your eyes open that you see the clearest.

—Dom Helder Camara

Though my soul may set in darkness,
    it will rise in perfect light.
I have loved the stars too profoundly
    to be fearful of the night.

—An Astronomer's Prayer

They also serve who only stand and wait.

—John Milton

For God alone my soul waits in silence.

—Psalm 62:1

O God, you are my God, I seek you, my soul thirsts for you.

—Psalm 63:1

two

the awakening hour

Themes for the hour:
praise and resurrection
joy and delight
the coming of the light

Dawn

Dawn breaks through night shadows. Fading darkness makes way for morning light. Golden rays exchange places with shining stars. All of nature leaps from the tomb of sleep and death. Everything stirs with renewed life. It is the hour of joy—a little resurrection. Rising from sleep, I raise high the chalice of my life. Dressed in robes of joyful anticipation, I enter this day with an open heart. This is the awakening hour. This is the hour of praise. "O medicine of dawn; O healing drink of morning!" Offering both words and silence, I join in the dance of creation. What will this day be like? Will I choose to walk through the hours mindfully? "To affect the quality of the day is the highest of arts," Henry David Thoreau tells us. And the mystical poet Jalaluddin Rumi reminds us, "The breezes at dawn have secrets to tell you; don't go back to sleep." Jesus says, "Stay awake."

> Shine your love on us each dawn and
> gladden all our days.
> —Liturgy of the Hours

When dawn threads its way through the darkened sky, it is time to rekindle our hearts. We awaken our delight in life so that at the end of the day we may voice the sentiments of the Emmaus disciples. When their eyes were opened, they recognized the One who journeyed with them on their pilgrimage through the day, that pilgrimage so full of questions . . . "Were not our hearts burning within us?" (Lk 24). Using slightly different words, this same question is displayed on the icon of the Emmaus journey that sits on my small altar: "Were not our hearts gradually catching fire?" If we move through this day with attention, perhaps we can echo these words in our Vespers prayer: Were not our hearts slowly being rekindled as we journeyed through the day carrying our lantern of Christ-light? This catching fire, this epiphany experience is also known as a theophany—an experience of God! From dawn to dusk these experiences of the divine surround us. Are we awake to their presence?

Some mornings I choose to choose life. There are mornings when I remember that it is not only the shining in the eastern sky that is rekindled at dawn. I remember that I am part of the shining. The spark of light in my own soul is rekindled, and I begin my day in glory. It is all about remembrance— remembrance of God and of good. Each morning as I look out my window I want to be awake enough to say, *Today I will remember to pause.*

At dawn when I arise, I like to face the east and wait for the coming of the light. I pray that I may be part of this rebirth on my pilgrimage through the new day. I sit or stand on my prayer mat and wait for the rising.

Morning is a call to our own resurrection, and so we reflect on what needs to rise in us. On some days we may need to awaken to joy. Or perhaps we need to pray that a positive attitude for our work will be resurrected. Sometimes it is compassion for a particular coworker, an aging parent, an alienated spouse, a troubled teenager, or a colicky child that is needed. If you prayerfully look into your heart, you will probably know what kind of resurrection needs to take place to honor the Awakening Hour.

Of course you do not need a prayer mat to praise the day's faithful return. In his book *The Illuminated Prayer,* which is a meditation on the Sufi masters, Coleman Barks quotes from the teachings of Bawa Muhaiyaddeen, "For those who have come to know God, the whole world is a prayer mat." These words hold much truth! On some days I go to the garden, to my sycamore tree, to the scriptures, or to chapel. One might even go into the streets of the city to find the great shining. It is remembrance of the Source of Life that is important. A compelling call from within bids us offer praise as we behold the face of God in everyone and everything.

From early Christian times the first hour of the day has been given over to praise. A spirit of joy permeates this hour. All is new and fresh. Light is beginning to encompass the darkness. We are summoned from sleep, called to wakefulness, invited to behold the face of the dawning day. This is the hour of resurrection. The very act of rising from sleep is our first antiphon. The lamp of life within us has been restored through the goodness of sleep. With our lamp lit, we go forth to give praise for the new day.

Dear as the gift of a new day may be, when we are passing through a great sorrow, we may understandably find it difficult to praise the dawning of another day. At times like this, the new morning may seem nothing more than a deeper drink of the bitter cup we are holding. I am convinced, though, that even in these dark times it is helpful to look to the heart for guidance. No life holds only joy and gladness; mixed in with delight is grief, doubt, discouragement. Yet there is something very special about joy. It is quite different from the happiness that can be short-lived and fleeting. Joy has the ability to live with and through the sorrows. Perhaps the reason for joy's persistence is hidden in a definition of joy that comes to us from the novelist Eugenia Price. "Joy," she says, "is God in the marrow of our bones." Joy is a deep well. If, in times of sorrow, we go down under the sorrow, we will discover that joy is still alive. Thus we will be able to raise high the chalice of our lives in any kind of weather.

Lauds! The very word means praise. Praise is not an easy word to describe. We come closest to understanding praise through experiencing it and perhaps sensing it taking up residence in our being. We feel as though we are being lifted out of ourselves toward some nameless mystery. We are drawn, like a magnet, to the sacred in every little thing.

John Ciardi's poem is a magnificent description of praise. Put yourself into this poem. Imagine yourself standing before a country pond at dawn. On the far side of the pond a heron suddenly takes flight. As you silently behold the heron's flight, the experience fills your being like a wordless song.

> What lifts the heron leaning on the air
> I praise without a name. A crouch, a flare,
> a long stroke through the cumulus of trees,
> a shaped thought at the sky—then gone. O rare!
> Saint Francis, being happiest on his knees,
> would have cried Father! Cry anything you please.
> But praise. By any name or none. But praise
> the white original burst that lights
> the heron on his two soft kissing kites.
> When saints praise heaven lit by doves and rays,
> I sit by pond scums till the air recites
> Its heron back. And doubt all else. But praise.
>   —John Ciardi

This is a poem to pray. For this poet it is obvious that words are not needed for praise. Praise is that which encircles one's entire being. What is essential is an awakened heart, a heart aligned with the joy or the sorrow of the moment.

At dawn I have the potential of becoming a living morning praise. With my glance I give praise. With my breath I give praise. With my grateful heart I give praise. In honoring the sorrows of life, I give praise. In celebrating the joy of the moment, I give praise. My desire to live this day well gives praise. With my voice I give praise. With my silence I give praise.

Even the skyscrapers give praise, as is seen in these tender words from the late Dom Helder Camara. This dear meditation is an icon painted with words. Once the words are spoken you can let them go and behold the beautiful image of praise it creates.

> I was afraid
> that with their blocks of concrete
> the skyscrapers might wound the dawn.
>
> But you ought to see
> how sensitive they are
> to the morning light,
> how they disarm
> and lose their cutting edge
> and steely soul!
>
> They too are caught
> in the irresistible spell
> of the holy hour
> when the whole natural world
> in rapture chants
> creation's hymn of praise.

—Dom Helder Camara

You, too, may have noticed how giant walls of concrete that penetrate the skies appear to soften in the wake of dawnlight as though they anticipate the world's weary ones soon coming into their concrete wombs to ply their skills. In the dawn moments they become shrines silhouetted against the amber sky, praying for their tenants.

Early one morning I sat before a small wood-burning stove. As I listened to the logs snapping and crackling, providing vibrant flames and welcoming warmth, I could suddenly see a tree burning in my fireplace. I saw it as it once was out there in the meadows, standing tall and strong, waving in the winds and storms, giving praise the way trees give praise. I saw the birds nesting in its branches, flying from limb to limb, singing from its top. After many years of being a tree, it became a gift of kindling for my stove. Later in the day I carried its gift of ashes into the garden where it could continue to give of itself that other things might grow.

Sitting before the flames that took the chill out of my hermitage on that brisk spring morning, reflecting on the tree, something welled up within me, and I understood this nameless *something* stirring through my being was praise.

I stepped outside, happily observing that reasons for praise were visible everywhere I looked:

- the crow with its glistening black feathers standing in the green grass surveying the meadow,
- the few brilliant yellow feathers in the tail of the flicker,
- the sun casting soft shadows on the hills,
- the old pecan tree pushing forth a few new green leaves,
- the freshness of the air after last night's storm,
- the community of toad stools that grew up in the night,
- the few cars moving down the country road,
- the angel-like mist rising from the pond,
- the sweet longing in my soul to raise high the chalice of my life.

Beholding all this beauty, I knew exactly what John Ciardi meant by, "Cry anything you please. But praise. . . . "

Learning to trust the healing properties of the beauty that surrounds me has become a spiritual discipline in my life. It takes practice, yet when I am faithful to the practice, I find it increasingly medicinal. There is a seed of praise in each of us. If it is watered with the daily practice of presence, it will find its voice in our lives and be good company for us on our pilgrimage through the day.

We are creatures of celebration. We celebrate with gestures of adoration, with words and songs of praise, and with silence. What is important, as the poet has emphasized, is that by whatever means, we offer praise. In order to praise we must be awake. The morning hour is about waking up. This waking up is infinitely more than just opening our eyes and getting out of bed. It is an awakening to the spiritual beings that we are and to the possibilities that await us as we move into this new day. Waking up requires practice. We practice remembering who we are.

I am a morning person. I don't always enjoy getting up; however, I like being up early. Getting up cheerfully in the morning is a spiritual practice for me. For this reason I set the clock of my heart as well as my alarm clock. It is important for me to wait for the morning light. Dawn is like medicine, and morning is a healing drink that I have to brew in my heart just as I brew my coffee.

How well I resonate with these words from Thomas Merton: "It is necessary for me to see the first point of light which begins to dawn. It is necessary to be present alone at the resurrection of Day, in the blank silence when the sun appears."

Although I am a morning person I am not necessarily a communal morning person. Before I go to the monastery chapel to sing praise with my sisters, I create a space of solitude for my personal morning rituals. I raise high the chalice of my life and make my intention for the new day. My morning intention usually includes the promise of trying to give joy to others.

In reflecting on the value of morning praise, it is helpful to remember that not everyone looks awake as they begin to wake up. Some time ago I had the opportunity to spend a few days in the country in Sweet Home, Texas, where I was able to rise with the rooster's crow and the sound of the Angelus bells ringing—an absolute delight to me. One morning as I sat quietly praying with my first cup of coffee, I looked up to see my friend sort of stumbling down the staircase. I took one look at her and jokingly said, "How can anyone who just heard the rooster crow and the Angelus bells ring look like this?" She looked at me as though I was a ghost and remained silent. Her silence put me in my place.

It is important that we respect the differences of others. Not everyone lives on my heart's schedule. Not everyone wakes up good to go. Not everyone wakes up wanting to give praise. Waking up in the morning is a process just as awakening to the gift of life is a process.

As we drink in the new life and light of the dawning day with all its joys and sorrows, we sense the goodness of being able to feel deeply. And so, in the spirit of the poet Kahlil Gibran, we can pray: "I arise at dawn with a winged heart and give thanks for another day of loving."

Prayers, Poetry, and Antiphons to Help You Celebrate the Awakening Hour

A Prayer Guide

Opening

> Set the clock of your heart for dawn's arrival.
> • Taste the joy of being awake.

Sacred Song

> The golden cradle of the moon
> is rising in the east,
> and all the things that croak and hoot
> and howl at night are silent now.

Moment before dawn
quietest of all quiet moments,
good medicine for the soul,
make plans to be there.

Set the clock of your heart,
breathe in the rays of dawn,
raise high the chalice of your life,
taste the joy of being awake.

O medicine of dawn!
O healing morning drink!
O new light from the skies!
O reason for my praise!

—Macrina Wiederkehr

(Portions of this song can be found on the CD *Seven Sacred Pauses: Singing Mindfully Dawn Through Dark*.)

Contemporary Psalm

Antiphon: No one knows what makes the soul wake up so happy. Maybe a dawn breeze has blown the veil away from the face of God. (Jelaluddin Rumi)

O Miracle of Dawn,
Radiance from the heavens!

With joyful silence, I receive
soft light of a new day,
light born from earth's turning.

O Medicine of Dawn,
healing are your morning rays.
I lift my face toward
the ointment of your splendor
as I become a morning prayer.

As Morning Blossoms,
I go forth to meet the great shining,
the dear unfolding of the day.
With the fading night
I begin a sacred dance
in the arms of your shining.

Encourager of Morning,
Soft glory of the new day,
I am tasting the joy of being awake.
Let your face shine on me
that, I, in turn may shine on others.

Repeat Antiphon.

Biblical Psalm Suggestions for the Awakening Hour

Psalm 19
Psalm 95
Psalm 147

Closing Prayer

Select the Prayer of the Hour below or another prayer in this section.

Prayer of the Hour

O Light of God . . .

Anointed by your morning light I lift my spirit to receive the gift of this new day. Open my eyes to the beauty that surrounds me that I may walk through this day with the kind of awareness that calls forth grateful living. In all of creation let me see the brightness of your face. Shine in my heart and on my life, filling me with joy, creativity, hope, and laughter. Draw me into the radiant glory of your presence and into the small lights of those with whom I live and work. Inspire me to take time for those who are discouraged. May I live with the kind of presence that enables others to feel at home. Great Dawn of God, hear my prayer.

Additional Prayers and Poems for the Awakening Hour

O Source of Morning's Brightness . . .

As new light streams out of the darkness, we open wide our hearts to the healing light of your Encircling Presence. Open our eyes to the opportunities this day has to offer. Surprise us with small joys and pieces of beauty scattered through the hours. O Beautiful Presence, help us this day to taste the joy of being awake. May this simple prayer come true in our lives today. Amen.

Morning Light . . .

You have come with your great shining, attempting to sing in a new day, but I have not the heart to receive your shining. I know it is the hour of resurrection and joy, and you are trying to wake up my gladness. Please respect my dreary mood. Your light comes into my darkness, yet my darkness remains unlit. All the same, I ask you to keep shining, and I will try not to be angry at your brightness. Perhaps at some moment during this day your glance of light will fall into my wearied soul. I do not ask you to stop shining, only this— understand my dark moment and be gentle with your light. O Morning Light, respect my darkness.

O Living Breath of God . . .

O Morning Song of Love, O you in whom we live and move and have our being!

We have been asleep too long. Heal the unseeing part of our lives. Lead us to our awakening places. Awaken us to the new light. Open the doors of our hearts, the windows of our souls, the walls of our minds. Awaken us to hope. Awaken us to joy. Awaken us to love. Awaken us to new insights. Make our hearts ready to receive the brightness of your presence. To you we give praise.

Dawn, Most Gracious Gift . . .

The words of Kahlil Gibran are sitting at the gate of my heart this morning: "To wake at dawn with a winged heart and give thanks for another day of loving." Words from Psalm 5 are also trying to get my attention: "In the morning you hear my voice; in the morning I plead my case to you, and watch." I don't always rise at dawn and watch for God, nor do I consistently awaken with a winged heart and give thanks for another day of loving. There are times when the wings of my heart remain folded; yet prayer still happens in me. There are mornings when I simply sit in silence trying to remember some of the things that need to rise in me:

—a tolerance for those who don't agree with me,
—a refusal to judge others,
—a willingness to forgive,
—greater effort to live with a non-violent heart,

—loving thoughts toward those who don't exactly
    dote on me,
—a calm and hopeful spirit in the midst of my
    anxieties,
—discipline in my daily personal prayer,
—attention and faithfulness in my daily work,
—a holy anger for injustice in our world.

As I remember these necessary risings in my life, the wings
of my heart slowly begin to unfold. All Praise to You, Giver
of the Morning!

The Blessing of Your Words as You Pause for Reflection

Gently lay your hands upon your lips, longing for the grace
to speak only words that are helpful this day. Remember the
words that you have already spoken. You cannot take them
back. Bless them and let them go.

O Word Made Flesh, stand guard at the gate of my
mouth. Be my voice this day that the words I speak will be
healing, affirming, true, and gentle. Give me wisdom to think
before I speak. Bless the words in me that are waiting to be
spoken. Live and abide in my words so that others will feel
safe in my presence. Surprise me with words that have come
from you. Oh, place my words in the kiln of your heart that
they may be enduring and strong, tempered and seasoned
with love and resilience. Give me a well-trained tongue that
has been borne out of silent listening in the sanctuary of my
heart. May my words become love in the lives of others.

Sweet Gift of Dawn

> Slowly comes the morning,
> softly comes the dawn,
> slowly and softly—softly and slowly.
> Dear Gift of Dawn, you come with rays of light.
> I call forth my joy to greet the dawn.
> In the marrow of my bones, I rejoice.
> From the center of my soul, I rejoice.
> In my heart of hearts, I rejoice.
> From the home of my body, I rejoice.
> With all my being, I rejoice.
> Dear Gift of Dawn, I rejoice.
>
> —Macrina Wiederkehr

Clothing Ourselves with the Day

> Out of darkness we come
> passing through dawn into day.
> Holding hands with dawn
> we clothe ourselves with light.
> We clothe ourselves with day.
>
> Out of the night we come,
> bathed and cradled in light,
> reaching through the dawn,
> we cover ourselves with day.
>
> Our beautiful bowl of life,
> so full of eternal questions,
> is filled to the brim with new light.

Morning light, be kind, help us find
peace of mind this day.

                        —Macrina Wiederkehr

Rise Early

Rise early
when morning darkness
still enwraps the trees.
Walk into the dark forest
with only your attentive heart.
Gaze toward the east,
take a deep breath, and wait.

After a short while you will see God
carrying a lantern through the forest,
bits of light bobbing up and down,
in and out, higher and higher,
the light climbs, spilling over
into the spaces between the leaves
and on into the world
beyond the forest.

Then the beautiful darkness
hands you over to the light.
It slips away reverently
into the bark of the tree trunks,
into the black earth,

into all those other countries
that wait for its return.

Lift your face to the daystar now.
Experience the coming of dawn.
Bathed in morning light, pray
that the lantern of your life
move gently this day
into all those places
where light is needed.

—Macrina Wiederkehr

Keeping Watch

In the morning
when I began to wake
it happened again
that feeling
that you, Beloved,
had stood over me
all night long
keeping watch. . . .

. . . that feeling
that as soon as I began
to wake,
you put your lips
to my forehead
and lit a holy lamp
inside my heart.

—Hafiz

A Book of Hours

> Every day is eternity
> labeled "Time."
> In the temple of God's worship
> it is the Hour of Prime.
> Before anyone saw Divine Splendor,
> creation chanted Lauds.
> and space had sung in stillness
> the Matins' praise of God.
>
> —Consuella Bauer, OSB

Antiphons for the Awakening Hour

The breezes at dawn have secrets to tell you; don't go back to sleep.

—Jalaluddin Rumi

To affect the quality of the day is the highest of arts.

— Henry David Thoreau

I arise at dawn with a winged heart and give thanks for another day of loving.

—Kahlil Gibran

Satisfy us in the morning with your steadfast love;
so that we may rejoice and be glad all our days.

—Psalm 90:14

It is you who light my lamp;
the Lord, my God, lights up my darkness.

—Psalm 18:28

Upon you I have leaned from my birth;
it was you who took me from my mother's womb.
My praise is continually of you.

—Psalm 71:6

Isn't it a splendid thing that there are mornings?

—Anne of Green Gables

Not knowing when the dawn will come I open every door.

—Emily Dickinson

Do not say, "It is morning," and dismiss it with a name of
yesterday. See it for the first time as a newborn child that has
no name.

—Rabindranath Tagore

I thank you God for this most amazing day: for the leaping
greenly spirits of trees and for a blue true dream of sky; and
for everything which is natural which is infinite which is
yes.

—e.e. cummings

We must learn to reawaken and keep ourselves awake, not by
mechanical aid, but by an infinite expectation of the dawn.
                                        —Henry David Thoreau

Joy is God in the marrow of our bones.
                                        —Eugenia Price

Joy is the echo of God's life in you.
                                        —Dom Marmion

Grant us what we need each day in bread and insight.
                                        —Neil Douglas-Klotz

Creator of the Dawning Sun, draw me with your eternal
energy. Filter your transforming glow through every inner
fiber of mine until I am transparent with the power of your
enlightening beauty.

                                        —Joyce Rupp

To God belongs the East and the West;
and wherever you turn, there is the face of God.
                                        —The Qur'an, Surah 2

No one knows what makes the soul wake up so happy.
Maybe a dawn breeze has blown the veil away from the face
of God.

> — Jalaluddin Rumi

There is something about embracing the day with the intimacy of a lover that makes one well again.

> —Macrina Wiederkehr

Bathed in morning light, pray that the lantern of your life
move gently this day into all those places where light is
needed.

> —Macrina Wiederkehr

The morning will surely come; the darkness will vanish, and
your voice will pour down in golden streams through the
sky.

> —Rabindranath Tagore

I cannot cause light. The most I can do is to put myself in
the path of its beam.

> —Annie Dillard

three

the blessing hour

Themes for the hour:
the coming of the Spirit
wind and flame, breath and blessing
strength and courage
the sacredness of work

Midmorning

In the middle of my morning's work I break for blessings: a deep breath, a glance out the window, a graceful stretch, a remembrance of God, a brief reflection on the nobility of work, an encouraging word, a grateful thought, a smile, a short prayer, a remembrance of who I am, a sip of freshly brewed coffee. I honor the wisdom of pausing. The day, still young, is fresh with the dew of possibilities. My work, too, is bright with potential. When I have the wisdom to step away from work momentarily, I am able to see it as a gift for the entire world. A short, refreshing pause can enhance my growing awareness that all work has the potential of becoming love made visible—a blessing. This is the Spirit's hour. I sense the overshadowing presence of all that is holy, and I remember that I am God's temple on earth, a channel for loving service. I hold out my hands to receive the blessings of the moment. When I remember to pause, blessings appear. I break for blessings.

When you work you are a flute
through whose heart
the whispering of the hours turns to music.
—Kahlil Gibran

It was in the middle of the morning when the Holy Spirit came upon the waiting disciples with gifts of courage and boldness for their new ministry in a birthing church (Acts 2:11–21). For this reason the apostolic church commemorated the joyful coming of the Spirit during the midmorning hour of Terce.

At this hour of the day we are still energetic. The day is young. In one of her poems Emily Dickinson proclaims, "I dwell in possibility"—truly an appropriate antiphon for this hour! *We dwell in possibility.* The opportunities of the day are numberless. In the midst of all these possibilities, then, we try to be aware of the Spirit's abiding presence. For this awareness to bear fruit we need to be able, at times, to stop what we are doing and remember who we are. To pause from our work for a few minutes, when some of us have just begun the day's labor, requires considerable trust. The day is so new and already we are asked to take a little breathing spell for the soul. The purpose of the midmorning pause, as in all the other hours, is a call to mindfulness.

Your work is for the benefit of the whole world. When your spirit mingles with Spirit, you are transformed into a temple of God. The house of God that you are gives a home to your mind, heart, soul, and spirit. It needs frequent renewal. It needs affirmation and blessing. Go deep into your temple. This is your real work place. Dwell there in silence that you may absorb the wonderful gifts of inspiration that wait for you in the darkness of your unknowing. In your contacts with people each day, you will be blessed if you remember that your work is your love poured out.

In this young hour of the day we prepare our hearts for the indwelling presence. We invite the breath of the Holy Spirit into even deeper places of our being. We open our souls to all that is windy and fiery. We long for constant renewal and strength so that as we continue our journey through the day, our love will be obvious in all we do. Our work will then be a blessing for all humankind. In some small way it will benefit the whole world.

It is a marvelous insight that our work is to benefit the larger world. In this age when, unfortunately, many people appear to be caught in the limitations of individualism, how good to be reminded that we are called to serve others, not just ourselves. Listen carefully to these words from one of the original hymns for the midmorning hour of praise.

> By every power, by heart and tongue,
> By act and deed, Thy praise be sung.
> Inflame with perfect love each sense
> That other's souls may kindle thence.

In this little prayer from an old hymn, we are asking for our love to be renewed so that other souls may be rekindled. Our reflective pause is for the purpose of restoring our own temple that those around us may find support and encouragement for their daily lives.

When I was a novice learning the monastic way of life, we were taught that midmorning prayer was a time to fortify ourselves for the day's battles. Although this way of thinking certainly holds some truth, I tend to look at it a little differently today. The word battle suggests confrontation and war. We live in a world with entirely too many battles, too much violence. Instead of focusing on fortification for battle, I like to place the emphasis on the consecration of our work. Rather than look at work as a punishment for sin, we can learn to look at work as a gift of love for the good of all creation. If we lost anything through sin, as the Genesis story implies, it was the ability to work with joy. It is true that, because of the obstacles we place in the way of grace, our work often becomes drudgery rather than blessing. Benedictines have always tried to honor the blessedness of work. This is where our focus needs to remain. How can we learn to work with joy and not disdain? How can our work be an honor rather than a burden?

The poet Kahlil Gibran offers us a jewel of truth when he tells us that work is "love made visible." He suggests that if we cannot work with love and joy, it would be better for us to sit at the temple gate and ask alms of those who know how to work with joy. This tender challenge is surely something to think about both when we are working and when we are pausing from work.

During your few minutes of non-doing, then, view yourself as a sacred temple. God's angels companion you on your pilgrimage through the day. You are never alone. Pausing to remember such truths changes the hours to gold. Once again Gibran speaks eloquently about work through these insightful words: "When you work you are a flute through whose heart the whispering of the hours turns to music." Of course, when we are in the midst of laborious tasks, we usually don't feel like a flute turning the hours to music. This is precisely why we need those healing pauses.

Most work requires the use of our hands in some way. It is an honor to use our hands to work for the good of others. It is a privilege to use our hands to restore and help build up creation. The psalmist prays, "O prosper the work of our hands" (Ps 90:17). In Chapter 48 of the Rule of St. Benedict we read, "When they live by the labor of their hands, as our fathers and the apostles did, then they are truly monks." On days when you remember to stop for a few moments at the midmorning hour, consider a simple blessing of your hands. At this midmorning pause, pray about the sacredness of your hands. This need not be an elaborate ritual. Simplicity often speaks with a quiet eloquence that is lost in elaboration. (One such simple ritual can be found in the prayer section of this chapter.)

The pauses throughout the day can be our teachers. If you are not accustomed to interrupting your daily work with prayer, you may find yourself questioning the value of this short break in your day's schedule. When you were a child, the first pause of your day was probably a little snack or kindergarten nap. Or perhaps it was your grade school recess that you remember. It is doubtful you questioned the value of that pause. When we grow up, we seem to have different ideas about the importance of recess. When those layers of responsibility, obsession, and control become part of our lives, they can kill a bit of our original pure spirit. We have traveled far since our school recess days. Perhaps a backward glance and a prayer to that child of long ago might be beneficial to the weary grown-up many of us have become.

As I learn the importance of pausing from work, I discover that these pauses become teachable moments for me. When I am faithful in taking little breathing spells at the various hours of the day, I ordinarily learn something valuable about myself. I have learned experientially that many of my creative thoughts actually slipped into my soul on another day—a day when I had the vision to pause for *being* in the midst of my *doing*. These inspired musings come and simmer in us until we become mindful enough to integrate them into our lives. Thus your midmorning prayer break can spiritually animate you and give you inspiration for your day's work.

Imagine you are sitting at the dawn of your workday, watching your creativity blossom. Rather than trying to grab the first blossom you see, spend time beholding that blossom and looking at it from all angles. Prayerfully reflecting on the first blossom of your day will awaken other ideas that are in the budding stage.

There are times when my attitude needs healing. Sometimes an insight pertaining to my relationship with a friend, coworker, or family member emerges, and I am able to see how this relationship is affecting my efforts to work with joy. A bitter heart is not good fertilizer for the fruit I want to bring forth from my day's labor. A reflective pause can help me evaluate how I approach my work and give me insights into how I might bring a more joyful presence into my workplace.

Each pause can be a blessing moment. Sometimes all we need is a freshly brewed cup of coffee. I have often observed people, including myself, chasing coffee cups around all morning—microwaving the coffee again and again and perhaps never really tasting it. Brewing a fresh cup of coffee and attending to it with the kind of presence that allows you to truly taste it is an act of mindfulness and a very good prayer. Thus on some days this kind of midmorning prayer might be something to consider: a cup of coffee with a moment of interior quiet, or a cup shared with a coworker.

In *The Music of Silence,* Br. David Steindl-Rast says that he associates the Blessing Hour with the monastery kitchen. I relate to this, for in the middle of the morning there is always someone in the kitchen preparing meals. The wonderful aromas and happy sounds are like midmorning antiphons. I particularly like to visit the kitchen on Friday mornings because that is when cinnamon rolls are baked. A hot cinnamon roll fresh from the oven is indeed a midmorning blessing worth the pause.

As we grow in mindfulness, we bring a new kind of presence into our day. Love and joy become frequent guests at our worktable. At times we may be tempted to berate ourselves because we have not completed everything on our morning work list. However, there is a better way to companion unfinished work. To access this better way, consider the word *equanimity.* It is an excellent midmorning word. The dictionary will probably tell you that it means *calm, composure.* I like the Buddhist teacher Joan Halifax's definition of equanimity. She suggests that it is the "stability of mind that allows us to be present with an open heart no matter how wonderful or difficult conditions are." To stand before both the difficult and the beautiful with an open heart will take some practice.

Let's apply this to our midmorning break. Whether we were very productive, slightly so, or even if we haven't gotten started on our workday, our spiritual being invites us to take a deep breath and stand before this hour with an open heart. Let us clothe ourselves with equanimity. Dwell in possibility. Sing the words of the chant that Velma Frye has created for this hour, thoughts gleaned from Joan Halifax and Emily Dickinson.

I stand before what is with an open heart.
And with an open heart I dwell in possibility.
I stand before what is with an open heart.

This little morning recess is a gift to yourself—a wordless prayer in the midst of your work. Spend a few moments of attentive breathing. Be aware of the state of your mind and bless the work of your hands. Be gracious with yourself and be grateful that you remembered to pause.

Even if you are out in the bustling traffic during this midmorning hour, you can still take time out for blessing. Turn off your cell phone, the radio, CD player, or anything else that is talking to you. Drive in silence. Spend a little time breathing. Be aware of the cars around you driven by people who, like you, sometimes are not sure they're going to make it through the day. These are people who have hopes, dreams, and fears like you. It costs little to send a blessing to them as you meet on the highway. Think about where you are going and why. Keep in mind the people you will be seeing when your car journey is over. Living with this kind of attentiveness takes practice, yet how delightful it is to be an unknown blessing in someone's life.

Prayers, Poetry, and Antiphons to Help You Celebrate the Blessing Hour

A Prayer Guide

Opening

O Spirit of the Circling Hours.
• Work through me that I may be your love poured out.

Sacred Song

Blessings. Blessings.
Blessings as the day unfolds, blessings of the
  morning,
Pausing in the fullness of the moment, our grateful
  hearts
 Sing a morning song on this holy ground.
 Sing a morning song to precious life all around.

Blessings. Blessings.
Blessings of the rising sun, blessings of the
    morning,
Pausing in the fullness of the moment, our grateful
    hearts.
    Sing a morning song on this holy ground.
    Sing a morning song to precious life all around.

Blessings. Blessings. Blessings of the morning.
                                        —Velma Frye

(This song can be found on the CD *Seven Sacred Pauses:
Singing Mindfully Dawn Through Dark*.)

Contemporary Psalm

Antiphon: I dwell in possibility. (Emily Dickinson)

Young, the day—awake, my heart.
Wide open and awake
to all the possibilities waiting
in the hours of this day.
O Spirit of the Circling Hours,
bless me that I may be a blessing,
Work through me, that I may be
your love poured out upon the earth.

Creator of all that is, be blessed.
Lover of all that is, be blessed.
Sanctifier of all that is, be blessed.
As you encircle our lives this day,
be blessed!

Repeat Antiphon.

Biblical Psalm Suggestions for the Blessing Hour

Psalm 67
Psalm 84
Psalm 121

Closing Prayer

Select the Prayer of the Hour below or another prayer in this section.

Prayer of the Hour

Abiding Spirit . . .

The fresh beginnings of this day embrace us as we stop for this midmorning pause. Bless the work that awaits us. Anoint our hands, hearts, and minds as we joyfully enter into the heart of this day. Make our spirits lucid, attentive, and open to all that can be. Breathe on us and strengthen us for our pilgrimage through the day. Come into our potential with your wind and flame. In Christ's name we pray.

Additional Prayers and Poems for the Blessing Hour

O Keeper of the Hours . . .

Sacred is the pause that draws us into stillness. Nourishing are the moments when we step away from busyness. Teach us the wisdom of pausing. Reveal to us the goodness of stopping to breathe. Bring to our memory the truth that we are the temple out of which you pour your gifts into the world. We are the temple from which you sing your songs. We are the temple out of which you bless. Enable us to listen to the renewal you are trying to bring about in us and through us. May we be reverent with each temple we meet and greet this day. May all the good that we long for come to pass.

O Blessed Spirit of the Hour . . .

The newness of morning lingers as the day wears slowly on. Lovingly behold the work that my hands, heart, and mind have achieved thus far. Receive it as part of my morning prayer. Let it be my love made visible. In this midmorning hour enlighten me that I may see the value of pausing to behold the blessings that surround me. Anoint my beginning efforts and give me a new heart to continue my journey through this day. When discouragement sets in, remind me that I dwell in possibility. In Christ's name I pray.

O Eternal Now . . .

I long to live in the present moment. I want to stop trying to control the hours so that new paths of inspiration are free to unfold within me. I want to remember that I have the potential to be a blessing in the lives of those with whom I live and work. Take my scattered thoughts, my fragmented moments. Breathe into them and draw them into your centered heart. Open my eyes that I may see the grace that waits for me in every moment. You are the Source of every moment's blessing. Teach me to live awake.

Anoint the moments of my day. May this prayer come true in my life.

O Spirit, Come . . .

Come with your transforming power. Breathe upon and into my thoughts and actions this day. Let my work be a labor of love. May those who come in contact with me feel sheltered and cared for. May I do or say some small piece of goodness that will help others feel affirmed and supported. Let your wind and fire move me into the places where I am needed. Let me become your breath so that I may assist you in breathing new life into places that are stale and unfruitful. Make me forceful and gentle, powerful and humble. O Spirit, Come!

O Holy One . . .

In you I live and move and have my being. Morning's bright beginning has worn away, and I am full of thoughts about the things I must accomplish this day. Remembering how you stole away from the crowd for personal prayer, I take a deep breath. I invite you into the ground of my being. I cannot leave my work right now but I can breathe. Breathe in me anew. I will follow your breath to the depth of my being. I will remember to pause. O Holy One, enter into the sacred space of my life and abide. Amen.

A Blessing Prayer

What is a blessing but a rain of grace
    falling generously into the lives of those in need;
    and who among us is without need?

May the Spirit touch your spirit in this midmorning
    pause.
May this day be a pathway strewn with blessings.
May your work this day be your love made visible.
May you breathe upon the wounds of those
    with whom you work.
May you open yourself to God's breathing.
May you honor the flame of love that burns inside
    you.
May your voice this day be a voice of
    encouragement.
May your life be an answer to someone's prayer.
May you own a grateful heart.
May you have enough joy to give you hope,
enough pain to make you wise.
May there be no room in your heart for hatred.
May you be free from violent thoughts.

When you look into the window of your soul
may you see the face of God.
May the lamp of your life shine upon all you meet
    this day.

                                    —Macrina Wiederkehr

The Blessing of Your Hands at This Midmorning Pause

Sit in your favorite chair, stand by a window, or choose some soulful place for this blessing prayer. Hold out your hands in gratitude for their many uses. Reach out and touch the things that are near you. Feel the texture of the things you touch. Think of some of the tasks you have done and will do this day. How important are your hands for these tasks? Now bring your hands to a comfortable resting place on your lap or held up in a gesture of praise.

O Source of Life, you lifted me out of the earth. From your hands I have come. I place my hands in the welcoming hands of your heart and pray for a sweet anointing in this midmorning hour. Anoint my hands with tender awareness. Anoint my hands with compassionate touch. Anoint my hands with sacred energy. Give success to the work of my hands this day. Help me remember my potential to reach out and touch things to life. Give me spirit hands. Fill my hands with insightful consciousness. Let me see with my hands the way those who are blind see. May all that I touch be transformed into an instrument of grace. O Holy One, anoint these hands and use them for healing all through the day. May it come to pass.

You may wish to use oil for anointing or water for cleansing and purifying your hands.

Morning's Sacred Spirit

Morning has a special Spirit.
She is a refresher of mind and heart.
Having practiced deep breathing
from the beginning of time,
each morning she breathes us into new love.
Into the temple of our lives she descends
and makes of us her temple song.
She breathes us alive each morning.

Spirit of the morning hours,
bless the work I have begun
that it may serve the larger world.
Transform my work
into a morning song of love,
a magical melody.
O refresher of mind and heart,
make me your temple song.
Breathe into my soul. Revive my love.

Spirit of the morning hours,
Breathe in me and through me
that I may be a morning blessing.

Inspire my creativity. Renew my heart.
Give success to the work of my hands.
As I pause to receive your holy breath
I embrace the Eternal Now.
With your breath, anoint my plans for this day.

Breathe me alive that I may become
a part of the melody of the universe.
Make me your temple song.

      —Macrina Wiederkehr

Love Made Visible

An artist would sculpt or paint you
and make of you an image
worthy of a gaze
intent enough
to behold all of your
wonder in just one glance.

A poet would fashion you into
a sonnet or a cinquain,
an ode or a sestina,
or maybe a ghazal
with just enough words
to utter you in,
to proclaim you forth,
sweetly.

But I have only this work
here, day after day,
to attend
and out of this daily
drudgery must lift
tired hands
and pull you
out of sheer possibility,

a task so difficult that
some days
my open heart
gapes
and nothing but the swish of
the Spirit's breath moving through
me could ever energize this effort
enough to call it a masterpiece.

—Beth Fritsch

Antiphons for the Blessing Hour

Sometimes the most important thing in a whole day is the rest we take between two deep breaths, or the turning inwards in prayer for five short minutes.

—Etty Hillesum

I dwell in possibility.

—Emily Dickinson

Work is love made visible.

—Kahlil Gibran

When you work you are a flute through whose heart the whispering of the hours turns to music.

—Kahlil Gibran

Carry into evening all that you want from this day.
                                        —William Stafford

Do you not know that you are God's temple and that God's
Spirit dwells in you?
                                        —1 Corinthians 3:16

Let your loveliness shine on us, and bless the work we do,
bless the work of our hands.
                                        —Psalm 90:17

Though my muscles may stiffen, though my skin may
wrinkle, may I never find myself yawning at life.
                                        —Toyohiko Kagawa

A cheerful heart is good medicine, but a downcast spirit dries
up the bones.
                                        —Proverbs 17:22

I will bless you, and make your name great, so that you will
be a blessing.
                                        —Genesis 12:2

When hard work soaks the shirt of humble folks, look about
you and you'll see angels gathering drops of sweat as though
gathering diamonds.
                                        —Dom Helder Camara

When love and skill work together, expect a masterpiece.
                                                 —John Ruskin

I don't know what your destiny will be, but one thing I know—the only ones among you who will be really happy are those who have sought and found how to serve.
                                              —Albert Schweitzer

Even if you have a lot of work to do, if you think of it as wonderful, and if you feel it as wonderful, it will transform into the energy of joy and fire, instead of becoming a burden.
                                        —Tulku Thondup Rinpoche

four

the hour of illumination

Themes for the hour:
commitment and passion
courage and faithfulness
healing, truth, and peace

Midday

This is the luminous hour. Everything is illumined by the brightness of the sun. There are few shadows. The intensity of the sun's shining is an excellent symbol for the enthusiasm I would like to bring to my work at this hour. The great shining touches growth seeds at the core of my being. The God of fire feeds my energy. Aware of the innate goodness of my life, an ardent desire to love and serve others is rekindled. I invite truth, authenticity, peace, and commitment to sit at my table. I long for the Beatitudes of Jesus to become my rule of life. Just as Jesus embraced the cross at this hour, I recommit myself to give my life away. I want to follow the example of Jesus in servant leadership. If I am to be a prophet of peace in a violent world, then I must practice living with a nonviolent heart. I must become peace.

> I came to bring fire to the earth,
> and how I wish it were already kindled.
> —Luke 12:49

During the noon hour all things are illuminated as the sun reaches its peak. It is the hour of no shadows. The brightness of this hour can serve as a significant metaphor for our spiritual lives. Surely there are moments when the brightness of God also reaches a peak in us. In moments such as these we experience the Divine Presence energizing us to live vital and vibrant lives on our planet.

Here are two quotes for your prayer in this hour of radiance. Jesus tells us, "You are the light of the world!" The poet William Wordsworth proclaims, "Trailing clouds of glory do we come from God." These words offer us a hidden invitation to accept God's glory as part of our inheritance. An awareness of the divine qualities in our own being enables us to shine on others, offering them the warmth and hope needed for daily living.

Of course not all of us are going to be trailing clouds of glory at this hour. Even though the sun has waxed to its highest peak and some are feeling energetic, others may experience their personal strength waning. How much spirit we are able to bring to this hour will probably depend on what sort of morning we've had and how long we've been at our jobs. The kind of environment we are working in will also color our daily moods and energies. The hymn for this hour makes reference to the heat of the sun and addresses the weariness we may be feeling at this midpoint in the day.

At this hour we look forward and backward, viewing about the same amount of day. The day is half empty of its hours; the day is half full of its hours. Do we find ourselves focusing on the fact that the day is half gone or feeling delighted that much of the day is still ours with vast opportunities to use wisely?

Are we filled with a healthy acceptance of ourselves at this time of the day? Are we able to stand before the hour with an open heart? Are we willing to make a commitment to move on into the afternoon with a hopeful and positive spirit? Or, are we battling what is sometimes called the noonday devil, the voice of discouragement? It is a nagging voice that gives us all sorts of untruths and bad advice: "You're not creative enough, successful enough, fast enough, good enough," and all the other "not enoughs" that tend to cripple and smother our enthusiasm.

In classical spirituality there is a word that is used to describe this inert, sluggish demeanor that sometimes robs us of our best selves. The word is *acedia*. It is a kind of spiritual apathy. It can overshadow our lives on all levels and thwart our efforts to remain joyfully committed to our work. We can be robbed of the vision needed to see that each of us has something valuable to offer our world. The poison of *acedia* can block our response to the great shining. It is not always just a passing mood; it can at times be a state of being. Although *acedia* can visit us at any hour of the day, I often experience its presence in my life at noontime.

Thus we see that this is also the hour of opposites: the hour of illumination and the hour of obscurity, the hour of energy and the hour of weariness, the hour of love and the hour of indifference, the hour of vibrancy and the hour of apathy, the hour of decision and the hour of uncertainty, the hour of commitment and the hour of discontent, the hour of faithfulness and the hour of *acedia*.

Even in this hour of opposites, it seems good to put the focus on illumination. In this season of the day when we are gifted with abundant light, why not focus on our potential to see? How faithful are we to the light? Will we choose to see the truth of who we are and who we can be for our world— our beautiful world so ravaged by violence and greed? If the light reaches our hearts, perhaps this will be the hour when our hearts break open—wide open, so open that we will be able to make the kind of decisions that lead to peace. This is the hour to become peace. Included in the original midday hymn for the monastic hours is a plea for peace: "Shed forth your peace upon the soul." If we open our hearts to receive the original peace of creation, we can be that peace.

In many monastic communities the angelus bells ring three times a day. The noon bell in particular is rung for peace, and the accompanying prayer is the Angelus. It is one of the church's lovely prayers of remembrance in honor of Mary's encounter with the angel when she is told that she is going to give birth to the Prince of Peace. I have vivid memories of praying the Angelus in the fields of my childhood farm. When the Angelus bells rang at noon, everyone stopped working and stood in silent prayer. This is a good hour to be reminded that each of us has the potential to give birth to whatever our world most needs. As Gandhi reminded us, "We must be the change we wish to see in the world." To that I add: We must be the peace we wish to see in the world.

In recent years as violence in our world intensifies, this midday hour has become a time, worldwide, to turn our thoughts toward peace. In my community, at the end of our noonday praise and just before we pray the Angelus, we recite these lovely words gleaned from a Hindu prayer for peace:

> Lead me from death to life,
> from falsehood to truth.
> Lead me from despair to hope,
> from fear to trust.
> Lead me from hate to love,
> from war to peace.
> Let peace fill our hearts,
> our world, our universe.

Deep as our longing for world peace may be, we know that peace must begin in our own hearts. For this reason we widen our thoughts about peace so as to include our personal lives, our attitudes, thoughts, and actions. At our midday pause, then, let us turn the eye of the soul to ourselves and check to see if we harbor any thoughts of violence in our hearts: violence toward self, family, community, coworkers, toward those who are different from us, toward any part of creation. We will never acquire world peace until we can learn to be peaceful creatures right where we are. We pray for nonviolent hearts.

The midday hour is a natural pause, as this is our customary lunch hour. However, so many people today use the lunch hour for business meetings. It has become a good time to tie up business deals, to evaluate and critique, to discuss future possibilities. "Let's grab lunch," we say. And grab it we do. In between sampling the cuisine or taking a bite of a sandwich we continue our work. This may be grabbing lunch, but it is not "coming to the feast."

This is not the kind of pause I am encouraging you to take, although having lunch as part of your prayerful pause can, on occasion, be a brilliant idea. The challenge, of course, is to keep work out of the conversation. Allow the lunch break to truly be a time of nourishment. Taste the food. Mutually bless one another as you share this meal. Linger on the conversation. Listen. Laugh. Be present. Encourage one another. Enjoy the moment.

Metaphorically speaking, this is a good hour to give support to others because the brightness of the midday sun can serve as a reminder that we are called to be a light for the world. Thus if others, being visited by the noonday devil, are bogged down with negative voices, our compassionate shining can awaken another voice that needs to be heard. Our noonday pause is a marvelous time to catch the rays of illumination and send away the negative voices. We need voices that will uphold, support, nurture, and sustain. After all, this is the lunch hour—a time of nourishment. We need fuel to continue our pilgrimage on through the afternoon. So whom do we invite to lunch?

Having recently reflected on the gospel story of Jesus telling the disciples to have courage, I am drawn to include courage as one of the special virtues to put on our guest list for this hour. The root of courage, from the Latin *cor*, means heart. This is the hour to take heart. Some of the other qualities we might want to consider as helpful midday companions are joy, a positive attitude, compassion, and acceptance. With all this good company at our noonday table, surely those negative voices will have less power. At this noonday hour let us take heart as we continue our pilgrimage through the day.

The noonday sun has healing resources. One of the traditional hymns for this hour addresses God as the truthful one. O God of Truth, we pray: You are the One who sends us new light at dawn. You watch over the changing seasons. Now it is noon and we experience the sun's fiery heat. The warmth of the sun has healing resources. In many therapeutic exercises, heat is used because of its restorative properties, and so we pray for health of body as well as peace of heart. We ask also that the effects of any harmful heat or flames of strife and violence be extinguished. In truth we are asking for balance and moderation in our lives, as we all know that our fiery passions can get out of control and inflict harm rather than accomplish the good for which they were created. It would seem remiss, however, to avoid mentioning that these fiery passions can also be used for good. We live in a world where the poor suffer from the greed of many and often from the corrupt, misappropriated power of those who ought to be speaking on their behalf. Since passion is one of the noonday themes, perhaps we need to take heart and see if we possess enough holy anger to assist us in helping to make positive changes in a world of so much injustice. We want to be angry enough but not too angry—angry enough to become a voice for the voiceless, yet not so angry that the warmth of our love and gentleness becomes invisible. How insightful the Sufi masters are in suggesting that when the power of love overcomes the love of power, there will be true peace on earth.

There are times when our midday pause might include going outside for a few minutes in order to allow the rays of the sun to shine upon us. A Vitamin D moment! Too much sun can be harmful, too little can also be harmful. The energy and power of the sun to assist in the growing seasons is obvious, as any gardener or farmer well knows. We, too, have our seasons of growth, and the sun is a marvelous star for us to feed upon. As you stand in the warmth of the sun, try to sense the sun's energy entering into all those places where you most need vitality and healing.

One of the chants suggested for this midday hour is a little prayer of affirmation. It is a promise to believe the truth about our goodness and potential. We are accustomed to the negative voices in our heads chanting out our flaws and weaknesses. The voice of this chant proclaims: I will believe the truth about myself no matter how beautiful it is. We are filled with a truth that cannot be contained. We can be the truth, the hope, the love, the peace that we long to see in our world. We can hold the warring nations of this world in our hearts and shine on them. We can hold in our hearts those who use power irresponsibly and cover them with Christ-love. Take heart! We can be healers in our world.

Prayers, Poetry, and Antiphons to Help You Celebrate the Hour of Illumination

A Prayer Guide

Opening

In this the hour of the noonday sun, let us bow to each other and pray for peace.
- Let us be the peace.

Sacred Song

In this, the hour of the noonday sun,
we raise our hands to the Peaceful One.
This is the hour to pray for peace,
for kindness and compassion to increase.

So let this be the hour of release.
Let us bow to each other and pray for peace.
Let this be our promise. Let this be our song.

We will be the peace for which we long.

Before we share our noonday meal,
our deepest hungers let us feel.
This is the hour for peace to flower.

Let us be the peace, Let us be the peace.
                                              —Macrina Wiederkehr

(This song can be found on the CD *Seven Sacred Pauses: Singing Mindfully Dawn Through Dark.*)

Contemporary Psalm

Antiphon: When the power of love overcomes the love of power, there will be true peace in the world. (Sufi Wisdom)

Take heart.
In this hour of opposites
between the waxing and the waning
we pause to remember who we are:
birth givers, peace keepers,
joy bringers, light bearers.

Take heart.
We are the light of the world.
In this hour of illumination
let us shine into the broken places
with our very own Christ-light.
Take heart.

We can be the peace,
we can be the healing,
we can be the Christ.
Trailing clouds of glory, we have come
from the brightness of God.

Take heart.
Our power to love will
overshadow our love of power.
In this luminous hour we will see
what we must see, and we will shine
because of what we have seen.

Repeat Antiphon.

Biblical Psalm Suggestions for the Hour of Illumination

Psalm 24
Psalm 33
Psalm 34

Closing Prayer

Select the Prayer of the Hour below or another prayer in this section.

Prayer of the Hour

O Luminous Face of God . . .

In this hour of no shadows, gather us into the guesthouse of your great heart and enable us to see all that waits for us in the brightness of your presence. Heart of Our Hearts, teach us to take heart at this high noon moment. Restore our courage and create in us nonviolent hearts that we may better serve your people. In the name of Jesus who asked us to take heart. Amen.

Additional Prayers and Poems for the Hour of Illumination

O God of All . . .

All peoples, all nations, all seasons, all years, all hours and days—you, who have invited us to love, hear our cry! Listen to our prayer. Make our spirits free, our hearts open, our minds healthy, our souls awake. Then we will be able to love as you have asked: with all our hearts, all our minds, all our souls. The *all* is frightening, yet in our deepest moments of truth we know that this is what we desire. O God of all, hear us.

In Christ's name we pray.

O Warmth and Energy of the Sun . . .

Beautiful reflection of divine light, shine on me at this noonday hour. Rejuvenate and invigorate me. Renew my commitment to the tasks of this day. Lead me to my courage. Warm what has grown cold in me. Energize all that has become lethargic. Enliven my growing moments. In the middle of this day help me to stand before my life with an open heart. In communion with all who have gone before me, I pray.

Truthful and Compassionate One . . .

Fill us with the splendor of your light. Give us the grace of your passion and compassion. Help us to burn with the fire of your love. Do not let our hearts become despondent. Do not let us surrender to the negative voices of the noonday devil. We ask for your courage, and that means we ask for your heart. Just as you have shone on us with loving presence we, too, would like to shine on your people that they may be blessed with new hearts and new vision. O God of so much giving, teach us to light tomorrow with today. In your healing name we pray.

The Angelus

This is a prayer that Catholics and other Christians have prayed throughout the ages. Traditionally it is prayed morning, noon, and night. It is an old prayer of historic beauty. When we pray a prayer frequently, of course, there is the danger of it becoming habitual with the possibility of losing some of its power and meaning. It may be helpful to approach these familiar words as if you are reading them for the first time.

The angel of the Lord declared unto Mary.
And she conceived of the Holy Spirit.

Hail Mary, full of grace, the Lord is with you.
Blessed are you among women
and blessed is the fruit of your womb, Jesus.
Holy Mary, Mother of God, pray for us sinners
now and at the hour of our death. Amen

Behold the handmaid of the Lord.
Be it done to me according to your word.

Hail Mary . . .

And the Word was made flesh.
And dwelt among us.

Hail Mary . . .

Pray for us, O Holy Mother of God,
That we may be made worthy of the promises of
    Christ.

Let us pray.
Pour forth, we beseech you O Lord, your grace into
our hearts, that we to whom the incarnation of
Christ, your Son, was made known by the message
of an angel, may by his passion and cross be brought
to the glory of his resurrection through the same
Christ our Lord. Amen.

An Angelus Reflection

The Angelus has recently taken on new meaning for me. I have been using it for *lectio divina,* or "sacred reading." This is a prayerful way of reading with frequent pauses for reflection. I suggest you pray this prayer slowly, pausing in the space between the lines.

Sometimes prayers that may seem old and outdated can, if you take them apart in this way, bring forth new images. Very simply, the Angelus asks that grace be poured into our hearts like water poured from a pitcher. It is the grace of God's life that we ask to be poured upon us. This grace is a reminder that just as an angel once brought the news of God's presence budding forth upon the earth in new ways, that same miracle of life continues as we discover that we are constantly being brought to new life through our daily dying. The following questions may help you gain new insights into the universality of the Angelus prayer.

- Name the angels who have brought you good news this week.
- Are you open to the presence of spirit in your life?
- How is the Holy Spirit conceiving in you new ideas, insights, and images?
- What is the promise of the Spirit for you?
- Can you see yourself as a messenger or servant of the Holy One?
- Can you hear God saying of you, "Behold her; behold him"?
- What kind of surrender is happening in you?

- Do you ever experience being called by a Word larger than your understanding?
- What is the newest Word that has become flesh in you, dwelling deep in the recesses of your being?

Illumination, Please!

Shine on me, oh Lord
for I am weary.
If I stumble this day
I fear I will never rise.

The work is overwhelming
the demands on my time many.
It's not supposed to be this way,
but how do I stop this merry-go-round
that is merry no more?

Feeling like I am falling
fatigue pulls me down.
I have no strength to
reach for the light
yet I know healing is there.

Oh passion, holy passion
where have you gone?
I miss your wild energy
for the noonday devil has come
to rob me of my joy.

Oh Great Shining
how can I pray for peace in the world

when there is little peace in my heart?

Oh Great Shining,
lift me out of this *acedia*
and back into your light,
Shine your love on me.

—Karen Ewan

The Truth

I will believe the truth about myself
no matter how beautiful it is:

I believe in my power
to transform indifference into love.
I believe I have an amazing gift
to keep hope alive in the face of despair.
I believe I have the remarkable skill
of deleting bitterness from my life.
I believe in my budding potential
to live with a nonviolent heart.
I believe in my passion to speak the truth
even when it isn't popular.
I believe I have the strength of will
to be peace in a world of violence.
I believe in my miraculous capacity
for unconditional love.

I will believe the truth about myself
no matter how beautiful it is.

—Macrina Wiederkehr

Antiphons for the Hour of Illumination

Only in embracing all can we become the arms of God.
—Coleman Barks

Shed forth your peace upon our souls.
—Monastic office hymn

We must love one another or die.
—W.H. Auden

Trailing clouds of glory do we come from God.
—William Wordsworth

I came to bring fire to the earth, and how I wish it were
already kindled.
—Luke12:49

Commit your way to the Holy One. Trust and God will act.
Integrity will rise like the sun, bright as the noonday will be
your healing.
—Psalm 37:5-6 (paraphrased)

You are the salt of the earth. . . . You are the light of the
world.
—Matthew 5:13-14

We must be the change we wish to see in the world.
                                        —Mahatma Gandhi

Probably the happiest period in life is in middle age, when the eager passions of youth are cooled and the infirmities of age not yet begun; as we see that the shadows, which are at morning and evening so large, almost entirely disappear at midday.

                                        —Eleanor Roosevelt

Be ablaze with enthusiasm. Let us be an alive burning offering before the altar of God.

                                        —Hildegard of Bingen

To become [human] means to have no support and no power, save the enthusiasm and commitment of one's own heart.
                                        —Johannes Metz

When the power of love overcomes the love of power, there will be true peace.

                                        —Sufi Wisdom

We are only here on the land for a few decades. Use every day to bring joy and not greed to our tired land so full of anguish.

                                        —Dorothy Stang, S.N.D. de N.

Assume a virtue, if you have it not.
                                        —William Shakespeare

What lies ahead of the human spirit can only be reached
through the slow process of living our way toward it.
                                        —Laurens Van Der Post

As the day grows, I, too, grow lighthearted, attentive, free,
patient, grateful, wise.
                                        —Macrina Wiederkehr

From the center of my soul, a flower grows inside me,
A love that makes me whole, a budding love that sets me
free.
                                        —Marilyn von Waldner

Peace is achieved by creating a world that is in alignment with
the Will of God, not the ego.
                                        —James Twyman

Come into the bedroom of our hearts,
prepare us for the marriage of power and beauty.
                                        —Neil Douglas-Klotz

five

the wisdom hour

Themes for the hour:
steadfastness, surrender
forgiveness and wisdom
impermanence, aging, maturing
death and transition

Midafternoon

The day is aging. Shadows lengthen as the light stretches toward evening. As the earth turns away from the sun, an ancient longing returns to my soul. It is a yearning for completion. It is a longing to put my house in order before the day ends. It is not just the loose ends of my work or my file cabinets or the laundry that need attention. My very being cries out to the living God, to the One who has gifted me with this good heart. I look to my heart for the wisdom to end this day well. I carry the answers to this day's problems deep within. As the day ends, I do not want the burden of bitterness to have a place in my life. If there is anyone I need to forgive, I seek advice from my inner teacher. I practice believing in my potential to let go of resentments. I pause to remember the lessons these hours have taught me. This day's troubles will end. When I meet them tomorrow, they may be tinged with blessing. I walk through the remaining hours of this day as I would walk through the last pages of a much loved book. I move through the hours present and aware that my work is a service for the larger world. I open myself to the love that comes from serving. Reflecting on the little deaths of this day, I become aware that at every moment I am dying to live. Love assists me in my desire to be faithful and steadfast in these last hours of the day.

Sustain me as you have promised that
I may live;
disappoint me not in my hope.
—Psalm119:116

Standing at the threshold of the evening, we embrace the lengthening shadows of midafternoon. In this brief afternoon pause we contemplate how we can put things in order as the day begins to fade. How can we sanctify these last hours of our work that we may end this day as we began, with the chalice of our lives lifted high?

This is another call to mindfulness. Look deep into your twilight soul and remember that this is the hour of reality. This is the hour of truth. All things are passing. This day, beautiful, frustrating, or productive as it may have been, will not last forever. It will fade into night and on into a new day.

At this midafternoon moment, most of you aren't dwelling in the twilight of your soul at all. You are probably looking at your watch and remembering how much you have to accomplish before day's end. There are, however, a few good hours left. You may not be able to complete the work at your side or in your hands today. Even so, if you bring a vigilant spirit of reflection to this work, you may be blessed with new and deeper insights. Moments of conscious pausing are good for the soul. Learning to stop before we are finished with a project can become a spiritual practice.

One of the themes of this hour is impermanence. Although this may sound negative, if you take time to reflect on the concept of impermanence, you may discover that it isn't a gloomy word at all. Who among us would like for this day never to end? Who among us would like to live here on this earth forever? And even though some of us may say, "I would," do we really mean that? We have here no lasting home. This truth is not necessarily bad news. When that reality penetrates our minds and receives our acceptance, we often start thinking and acting in ways we would never have dreamed possible. When this learning takes place in our lives, it isn't all that difficult to stop what we are doing for a moment and ponder another dimension of life.

In the midst of our work, then, we begin to live with an awareness that although, hopefully, what we are *doing* will be of service to our world, it is our *being* in the world that is the essence of all we do. Our doing flows out of our being and that is why it is necessary for us to learn to pause.

When you are alert, you will notice that different hues of light move through the day with you. The hymn for midafternoon addresses God as creation's secret force traveling with us as our guide through the changing patterns of light. With the lengthening of shadows, we do not have the brightness of the noonday light to rely on. It is time to search for the luminosity that comes with the wisdom years. In this hour of shadows it is our inner light, which is also known as insight, that comes to our assistance.

Day's end is symbolic of life's end. The gift of life on earth will not last forever. In the Rule of St. Benedict we are asked to keep death daily before our eyes. This is not intended in a dismal sense. It is a loving reminder of the beautiful fragility in the lives of human beings here on earth. An honest remembrance that all things are passing can help us grow in gratitude for all of creation and for the hours of the day. This awareness can enable us to live joyfully in the present moment.

For those of you working eight-to-five jobs, this may appear to be a badly chosen time to reflect on death. However, the time to meditate on death is not when we are dying. In the evening years of life we are more willing to look at the reality of death. Remembering the impermanence of all things in this prelude time before the dying day is actually good timing. Some questions to ask at this hour might be: To what am I tenaciously clinging? Where do I need to loosen my grip? Maybe it is the day itself that you don't want to let go of. Perhaps at this hour you are being called to wrestle with the question of why there is such a driven aspect to your work. Our driven state is a disorder that cries for attention. Just what is it in our bodies or in our society that causes us to live as though there were no tomorrow? Perhaps our driven condition has something to do with the difficulty many people experience in trying to live in the present moment. It is true that, for the most part, no one applauds us when we pause from working. The applause often comes when we are working overtime, when we are going beyond the call of duty. There may be times when working beyond the call of duty is admirable, but making a lifestyle of this manner of working borders on compulsion and may be more of a sickness than a blessing.

You have an inner teacher who can act as a guide for you concerning the fears you may have relating to impermanence. Try to identify your fear. Is it fear of letting the day go, leaving work undone, losing your youthful vitality, living in the present, pausing for reflection? Is it fear of living without excitement and drama? Is it fear of dying?

This inner teacher is known as "the Old One." He or she abides in the core of your being. In some ways I've always known about the Old One. I was first able to give it a name when I read an essay by Michael Ventura, a Los Angeles writer. In this essay Michael is visiting the various birthdays of his life. As he crossed the fifty mark he ponders the reality that while in ancient times to be old was a mark of honor, in today's society that respect has turned to dread and even shame. For many people, so much energy revolves around staying young or at least looking young. Certainly "the Young One" needs to be treasured, nurtured, loved, and cared for. The young person has a vibrancy that many of us middle-aged and older ones gaze upon wistfully and sometimes regretfully. We feel, at times, that we have lost some vital aspect of our personality. Sometimes we become homesick for our youthful days. We need to remember, though, that we also have a unique gift to bring to the younger generation. That gift is an acceptance of the reality that every age is beautiful and that our growing awareness of the impermanence of all things can gift us with wisdom. Those who are young often seem reluctant to reflect on the reality that they are going to die. When the young find themselves faced with the reality of death, they prefer to turn away their faces from that truth. This is precisely why they so desperately need to honor the Old One who already lives within them.

The Old One has lived with us since birth. There have been times, even in our youth, when the Old One in us has momentarily shown its face, and we trembled with an awe and nostalgia that we couldn't quite grasp or make our own. In the evening hours of life, hopefully we can finally turn unashamed to that *old one,* listening to its wisdom. So at this hour of the day when we are in the vestibule of evening, why not take a few moments to sit at the feet of the Old One and listen to the silence? The Old One often speaks in silence, knowing that in an abundance of unnecessary words, as the Rule of St. Benedict also teaches, we do not find the Love our hearts seek.

This is the hour of life when we become less afraid to reflect on death—the hour when we may even begin to realize that death and life are related. The Indian poet Rabindranath Tagore assists us in seeing more clearly how death can be our teacher in this exquisite poem. The poem begins with a question:

When death comes to your door
    at the end of day
        what treasures
            will you hand over to him?

Perhaps we could ask the same of the dying day: What treasures have we harvested from our day's work? When the day comes to an end, what gifts do we have to share with our sisters and brothers of the world? "To affect the quality of the day," Henry David Thoreau reminds us, "is the highest of arts." How have we affected the quality of this day?

Returning to Tagore's poem, take note of the positive tone with which the poet answers his own question.

I'll bring
    my full soul before him.

I'll not send him away empty-handed
    the day he comes to my door. . . .

All the treasures I've gathered
    during my lifelong preparation
        I'm now arranging for the last day
           to give it all to death—
                the day he comes to my door.

The poet's voice sings with acceptance, equanimity, and wisdom. Indeed, in these words, one senses that dying is an art. Death is being offered a bouquet of life.

And what about us? What are our feelings about death? Do we know how to die? Do we know how to let our loved ones die a natural death? These are not easy questions. We might want to turn to the tribal peoples of old for guidance. Aboriginal peoples were community oriented. They valued one another immensely, yet they did not try to keep their loved ones alive forever. They allowed them to die a natural death. Their dying was a celebration of life. Of course we can argue that they didn't possess the quality of life we enjoy because they were lacking in the educational background, resources, and medical knowledge we have today. That may very well be true, but they possessed a different kind of quality of life. One truth to consider about the elders in tribal living is that they didn't spend their lives trying to look eternally youthful. There was no such thing as anti-aging cream. There was a natural wisdom in their living that was partially the result of being able to live one moment at a time.

The ancients had a different relationship with time than most of us have. Time was not an enemy with which to do battle. How often we speak of time as fleeting and fleeing. We are forever losing time or wasting time. We try to manage and organize our time. We are multitasking to get more into the hours of the day. For the elders of our historic past, time was more of a loving companion. In this book I am trying to paint an icon of time as a companion, friend, and mentor. We stop at each station of life. Each station in life is one of the hours—one moment in time. We pause to contemplate the beauty of the hour. There is, of course, clock time (*chronos*), which we need to help us appraise, calculate, and give some rhythm to the hours of our day. There is also soul time (*kairos*), which is a sacred moment of readiness for spiritual growth. When our days become eaten up with *chronos,* it is time to embrace *kairos.*

With the approaching evening it is time for giving and for forgiving. Giving and forgiving are kindred spirits. Forgiveness is one of the virtues of this hour. When you forgive, you give life back to the other. When you withhold your forgiveness, you injure the life of the other. When you forgive, you lift a burden from yourself and the other. If you wait to forgive until the other person is fully aware of his or her wrongdoing, you may wait too long. Your gift of forgiveness may very well be the medicine that the other needs to heal, and in your act of forgiving you, too, will experience healing.

As we look toward the dying day it seems fitting to reflect on that ancient proverb, "Let not the sun go down upon your anger." Or, "Let not the sun descend on bitter hearts." The words of Saint Teresa of Avila, in mentoring the sisters in her community, also invite us to put our house in order before the close of day. "My Sisters," she says, "there is no evil greater than being ill at ease in your own house." We desire to be at peace within the temple of our being as well as the households in which we dwell. We want to close this day, as we began, with the chalice of our lives raised high. This day has been a day for giving our best self to our work. It has been a day for remembering that our work benefits the whole world. It is good to take a little soul time to prayerfully put things in order as the day begins to die. We will never have the completeness we long for when we reach the hour of the Great Silence (Compline) if our hearts are crowded with leftover anger and grudges. For this reason we begin early with our plans for the great surrender of forgiveness. We strive to forgive our colleagues and ourselves for the weaknesses and mistakes of the day. With the love that befits our deep souls, we put things in order as the day begins to close.

Prayers, Poetry, and Antiphons to Help You Celebrate the Wisdom Hour

A Prayer Guide

Opening

> We stand before the dying day
> • Offering our bouquet of life.

Sacred Song

> Put everything in order
> as day begins to fade.
> All things are passing,
> moment by moment,
> breath by breath.
> All things are passing,
> moment by moment,

birth to death.
Take off that cloak of fear,
the divine strength you seek is here,
and you know you are dying to live.
You know you are dying to live.
So put everything in order
as day begins to fade.

—Macrina Wiederkehr

(This song can be found on the CD *Seven Sacred Pauses:
Singing Mindfully Dawn Through Dark*.)

Contemporary Psalm

Antiphon: We seek to live a more contemplative life,
so that we will not have to wait until we are dying
to learn to live. (James Finley)

O Soft Light of the Waning Sun,
the evening of life is on its way.
At day's end, guide us to look within.
Usher us into the wisdom hour.
Teach us the grace of listening.
Reveal to us the art of dying.
Show us the face of God.

O Soft Light of the Waning Sun,
we stand before the dying day
with our bouquet of life:
sweet abiding, deep listening,

holy surrender, forgiving heart,
tender love, quiet joy,
gentle spirit, sacred presence.
This is our gift to those
with whom we share our lives.

Repeat Antiphon.

Biblical Psalm Suggestions for the Wisdom Hour

Psalm 71
Psalm 90
Psalm 138

Closing Prayer

Select the Prayer of the Hour below or another prayer in this section.

Prayer of the Hour

O Ancient Love . . .

In the evening of our lives send calming angels to shelter us and take away our fears. Lead us to "the Old One," who lovingly waits for us to embrace our deepest and truest selves. Teach us to die before we die so that our final death will be a great healing, drawing us into deeper life. Show us the face of surrender that we may know at the end of each day what to let go of and what to keep. O Soft Light of the Waning Sun, teach us the beautiful art of dying. Fill us with your own wisdom. In Christ's name we pray. Amen.

Additional Prayers and Poems for the Wisdom Hour

O Wisdom of the Years . . .

Give us the grace of tender seeing. Help us to recognize and honor the wise one who lives at the core of our being. May we always be open to being taught. May we be able to let go of our work at the end of the day. May we learn to bless and affirm each person who passes through the hours of our day. May we lose our fear of those things which are transient. May we learn the art of living well and dying well. Teach us to end the day slowly, thoughtfully, gracefully. Soften the driven part of us that we may learn to relax and offer all we are and all we do as a bouquet of life at the close of each day. In the name of the Old One who lives in us, we pray.

O Searcher of Hearts . . .

As the shadows lengthen, search my heart for any traces of bitterness. Reveal to me all that keeps me from living with a free and unburdened heart. Empty me of all that is false and binding. Let me walk into the twilight hour of this day with gratitude. May I be liberated from all resentments. As this day dies I, too, shall die. I offer the work of my hands as a bouquet of life for the good of all. O searcher of hearts, at the end of this day present me as a gift for the entire world. May it be so.

O Source of All that Is Undying . . .

Receive my prayer. In the midst of so much that is ephemeral, I sometimes experience the rising of fear. Why do I become fearful in the shadows of that which is passing away? O Eternal Beauty, even that which does not linger long has a lasting place in my soul. Closing my eyes I behold within my soul's memory the things that once gave me joy. They linger on as sweet shadows of yesterday. In the midst of all that is passing away I sense a deep truth in my life that will never die. Source of that which is undying, allow me to be a joyful memory in the lives of others. O let it be.

To the Old One Who Lives in Me I Pray . . .

O ancient wisdom so deeply rooted in the ground of my being, anoint me with your wise knowing. As I look toward day's end, let me draw energy from your insight and good judgment. Open my eyes to the riches you have gifted me with this day. Help me gather it all in as a bountiful harvest. Let me sit at your feet and learn from you how to live and

die, how to give and forgive. O teach me wisdom. May it
come to pass.

The Old One

When I look back on this day
do I see

a sea of smiling faces
because I smiled first,
a forest of soul-filled conversations
because I took the time to listen,
a world of heartfelt hugs
because I opened my arms,
a field of hopeful hearts
because I used words of hope?

I see the Old One
dwelling deep inside.
I feel the Old One
inviting me to pause,
offering me the wisdom
that flows through my being,
the wisdom I already possess.

—Karen Ewan

O Impermanence!

Standing in my evening vestibule
wrapped in fading light

I push Chronos out the door firmly.
Your time is up, I say
as I usher in my dear friend Kairos,
pulling her into a welcoming embrace.

Goodbye clock time,
tick-as-you-must time,
Hello grace time,
Swirling-spirals-of-sense time.
Set-my-heart-free time is
past due today.

Come in!
I know you cannot stay long
and I so yearn
to spend some moments wisely
in your comforting company.

Advise me,
hour of wisdom's beginning.
Impart your secrets of forgiveness,
Drench me with your sacred silence.
Remind me of my own steadfast spirit!

Reveal my task for this hour,
And then be on your way,
dear friend!
Move swiftly as I long
to clothe myself in your certainty,
to detain you forever as my faithful guide.

But alas, even you must be surrendered!

                                    —Beth Fritsch

Antiphons for the Wisdom Hour

Teach us to count our days that we may gain a wise heart.
—Psalm 90:12

Sustain me as you have promised that I may live; disappoint me not in my hope.
—Psalm 119:116 (NAB)

We seek to live a more contemplative life so that we will not have to wait until we are dying to learn to live.
—James Finley

Light tomorrow with today.
—Elizabeth Barrett Browning

A tiger dies and leaves its skin; a person dies and leaves his [or her] name.
—Korean Proverb

Nothing in this life that I've been trying could equal or surpass the art of dying.
—George Harrison

I loved her [Wisdom] more than health or beauty, and I chose to have her rather than light, because her radiance never ceases.

—Wisdom 7:10

Death belongs to life just as night belongs to day, as darkness belongs to light, as shadows belong to substance . . . death belongs to life.

—Rabbi Alvin Fine

Who knows what is beyond the known? And if you think that any day the secret of light might come, would you not keep the house of your mind ready? Would you not cleanse your study of all that is cheap, or trivial?

—-Mary Oliver

I don't know what your destiny will be, but one thing I know—the only ones among you who will be really happy are those who have sought and found how to serve.

—Albert Schweitzer

It's too bad dying is the last thing we do, because it could teach us so much about life.

—Robert Herford

I have tried to make a day-by-day decision that I want to live joyfully. I want to be good news to other people. I'm going home like a shooting star.

—Thea Bowman, F.S.P.A.

We die daily. Happy are those who daily come to life as well.

—George MacDonald

This is the lesson of age—events pass, things change, trauma fades, good fortune rises, fades, rises again, but different.

—Mary Oliver

six

the twilight hour

Themes for the hour:
gratitude, praise
serenity, mystery
the lighting of the lamps

Evening

At dusk, when twilight enfolds me and the fading sun leaves behind a wake of color, I stand in the gloaming. One hand cradles daylight, the other welcomes night. In this Vespers hour I sense a very thin veil between heaven and earth. Moving into this mystical twilight time of the day, I reflect also on the twilight time of the soul. As I symbolically take off my work clothes and put on the robe of prayer, my soul ages like good wine. The old soul that has always been a tenant in the ground of my being hums quiet melodies to me at day's end. It is a melody of gratefulness, the music of gratitude. In the evening of life, when I am growing towards vigilance, I am able to listen from a deeper place within my being. I am given greater access to the divine mysteries. I accept the blessings and difficulties of this day as part of my life's curriculum. I bring to my evening prayer all the small ones of this world who have no voice of their own, knowing that I must learn to be a voice for the voiceless. I rejoice in the opportunities to love that this day has offered me, giving thanks for a day well spent. Like a magnet, I am drawn into the spiritual heart of my praying community. I sense the breath of God moving through me. All around me the lamps of evening are being lit. I, too, light my inner lamp of love. Clothed in the quiet light of evening I enter the Vespers song of praise. As I become a part of this twilight music, I am aware that the more deeply I enter the song of praise the more truly I become the song. Love finds my heart open and I am at peace.

———————

In the twilight of life, God will not judge us
on our earthly possessions
and human success,
but rather on how much we have loved.
—John of the Cross

Vespers, the much loved evening prayer of the church, has been prayed throughout the ages by monastics and non-monastics alike. This hour has a mystical quality about it. Although our varying lifestyles and schedules decide just when our workdays end, each of us, in our own way, must learn to listen to the prayerful call of the sunset hour.

One of the dearest moments of my monastic day is when we gather for evening prayer. The bell rings, and suddenly, one by one, we draw together around the altar where we celebrated morning Eucharist. As I look at the circle of my sisters and behold their faces, I am moved by our faithfulness. It is not hearing the bell that brings us together; it is listening to the call. Hearing the bell and listening to the invitation are two different experiences. Some questions to ask ourselves as we gather: Are we here because we heard the bell or because we listened to the call? What is the invitation of this hour?

To what are we called? Why do we stop working at the end of the day? Which encounters of this day have rekindled our hearts? For what are we grateful? Inviting a few personal questions into our lives can be a good preparation for our evening praise.

Sometimes we want to be there; sometimes we don't. At times the psalms we are chanting touch our spirits deeply; at other times they do not inspire us at all. We come because we have been invited to close our workday with prayer. We have gathered in community to give thanks for the blessings of this day.

In monastic life, Vespers comes at the end of our workday. It is time to put most of our work tools away and turn our thoughts to making peace with the day and with one another. In our midafternoon prayer we prayed: Let not the sun go down on bitter hearts. Now that the sun is departing, we may be drawn to check the condition of our hearts.

For many of you in the workaday world this may be the end of your day job, but more than likely a myriad of other little jobs await you: transporting children to various places, caring for elderly parents, coaching little league, picking up groceries, preparing meals, working in the garden, and on and on the list could go. Thus each of you will need to find your own Vespers path. The Vespers hour invites you to pause and remember who you are: Caretaker of Earth, Temple of Divine Light. Here are a few questions to ponder on your way home from work. These questions can serve as a gentle assessment of your day, drawing you into a deep gratitude. The questions that come out of your own heart, however, are the essential ones.

- What has been the greatest blessing of this day?
- What one accomplishment can I smile over?
- Is there an unfinished task that is taking away my sense of fulfillment? (If so, bless it with the promise that you will attend to it tomorrow.)
- Will I choose to relax in some way this evening?
- Am I able to look with compassion on the faces of those who have been part of my workday?
- John of the Cross says, "In the evening of life we shall be judged by love." How well have I loved this day?
- Is there anyone I need to make peace with before the day ends?

The journey away from work back to your home is a transitional time. All those incomplete projects may want to come with you. As you prepare to leave your work place, is there a certain contentment you are able to bring with you? Perhaps you will need to practice finding that contentment on your way home.

Often at day's end the things that must yet be done form a circle around us and vie for our attention. We long for the rooms of our hearts to be at rest and find instead anxious, petulant hearts. We are, however, in charge of our attitudes. We have the power to transform fretful hearts into grateful hearts. Gratitude is one of the themes of the Vespers hour. If you search out reasons to be grateful, you may be amazed to discover that your gratitude room is overflowing. This honored guest is a healing companion, always available to you. Gratitude is like incense. It ascends and flows out as a sweet fragrance to everyone. A heart filled with gratitude is a heart filled with the incense of prayer. The prayer of gratitude guards us from negativity! We practice being grateful for what we've accomplished, leaving what is unfinished in Eternal Hands.

Undoubtedly there will be days when you are tempted to bring some of your work home. Perhaps the great challenge here is that you keep careful watch over this tendency so that it does not become an everyday practice. If you want to be attentive to your soul, you simply must find ways to honor your need to acquire a sense of rhythm in your life—some kind of balance in your work, leisure, and prayer.

On a partially cloudy day the Vespers hour can be one of exquisite beauty as color flames forth in all directions. This twilight hour has a luminous quality to it and has been treasured throughout the ages as a time to light the lamps of evening.

With one hand we cradle the waning daylight; with the other, we embrace the approaching night. In this gloaming hour it seems as though there is but a thin veil between that which is divine and that which is earthly. In the Celtic Christian tradition, places where two worlds meet are called thin places. For me, sundown is one of those thin places that the Celtic peoples speak of so endearingly. It is a moment in time when heaven and earth almost touch. The veil separating them is so thin that if you are able to be wholeheartedly present, with no distractions, you can lift that veil momentarily and see the face of God. When I am fortunate enough to be able to pray Vespers with the departing sun, I experience the intimacy of this hour. As the sunlight softens I cherish the opportunity to stand in this twilight thin place with a vigilant heart. The magical moment between day and night is my soul's favorite hour. At this mystical time of the day I yearn for spiritual eyes to see the face of God.

Katherine Olson writes about how the hour of sundown was a constant consolation in a period when she was fresh out of the university, looking for a job, and anxious about the future. Even in the heart of her turmoil she claims, "The flow of day into evening was a constant reminder for me of the divine energy behind the onset of every twilight. . . ." She became aware that many of the people who traveled with her were totally oblivious to this miraculous falling of the day into the night each evening. Commenting further on the enriching experience of consciously receiving day's end with its enchanting array of colors, she says:

> Looking back on these past few months of learning and doubting, I now see beauty in the way the night crawls unfailingly toward us all, perhaps pitying those who fear it, not slowing for those who relish it. Daylight, I know, will come again soon enough, and this makes the red and white lights that dance the night skies seem beautifully choreographed. I know now deeply and from experience that the "sun knows when to set" (Ps 104:19).

In this age when so many people struggle to find ways to spend quality time with one another, it would, indeed, be a blessing to share a few "Emmaus moments" at the end of your day. (The Gospel of Luke, chapter 24, recounts how the risen Jesus walked with two of his disciples on the road to Emmaus and lifted their spirits as he explained the scriptures to them. They finally recognized him in the breaking of bread together.) To break the bread of our lives with one another through any form of sharing is prayer. To quietly behold the Vespers colors of a sunset with a loved one is prayer. Why not on occasion ask a family member or friend to reflect with you on your mutual pilgrimage through the hours? Sharing with another your blessings and concerns is a kind of bread-breaking moment. There are many ways to feed one another on our journey through the day.

Being attentive to the hours is an enriching spiritual practice. This kind of radical attention, of course, is not easy and requires much conscious effort and prayerful intent. Many people's workday is so demanding and hectic that finding time at the end of the day for any kind of spiritual integration is a tall order. It may be helpful for us to look at ways that others have found to make the spiritual practice of pausing more achievable in their lives. The few examples below offer us little glimpses into the spiritual practice of others.

A woman who is a nurse at a large hospital takes her sacred pause in this way. On her way home from work she has made a practice of stopping, at least twice a week, to take a leisurely walk through a park.

Another person describes how he turns off the radio and his cell phone when he gets in his car. On the drive home he tries to see people rather than traffic—people with worries, concerns, and joys akin to his own. In prayerfully connecting with all these people going home at the end of the day, he experiences a little communion right there in the midst of the traffic.

A therapist speaks of how, at the end of the day, she reverently visualizes her clients for the next day, seeing not just a patient's chart filled with progress notes and directives but a person full of hopes and fears, dreams and possibilities. A hand laid on a patient's chart becomes a reflective pause, a prayer.

One of my colleagues shares a story about someone who has found a way to honor his need for some down time after work and yet be present to his family. He has made an agreement with the family that when he gets home in the evening he has time to take a shower, get into casual clothes, and perhaps read the paper. After this he is ready to enter into whatever needs the family might have, from romping on the floor with children to watering the garden or mowing the yard.

A poet, Patricia A. Lunetta, poignantly describes one of her reflective pauses in a poem entitled "The Visit." It is her last visit with Margaret. We don't know who Margaret is. She may be a friend in a nursing home or in a health care facility. She may be a family member or relative. The poet speaks with such intimacy of rubbing Margaret's feet, "touching death and bumped out with bunions." You sense that she leaves Margaret that day full of weariness and love. Her poem ends with the description of what I am calling a Vespers moment.

> . . . As I drive home on a narrow curving road,
> someone tailgates, itching to go faster,
> not knowing he's flesh and fragile.
> Slowed by sadness and sick of pressure,
> I pull onto the gravel shoulder, let him
> shoot by, and on my right
> catch sight of a great blue heron
> standing tall and still in the aisle

made by two rows of towering trees.
Like a priest in feathered robes,
he bows his head three times
before an altar of mountain bluffs. It's dusk,
and the moon, just rising, illuminates
his wings as they open in benediction
for evening flight. His parting call:

"Stay awake, Holiness
may spread its wings for you
at any moment."

—Patricia A. Lunetta

As you reflect on Patricia's lovely poem, make your own plans for celebrating the beauty of the twilight hour. How will you pause to see the face of God after your hard day's work?

Prayers, Poetry, and Antiphons to Help You Celebrate the Twilight Hour

A Prayer Guide

Opening

My eyes scan the horizons of your goodness.
• The incense of gratitude rises as an evening prayer.

Sacred Song

A thousand colors is your face
    embracing us with waves of grace,
and as the day star now departs
    your glance of light fills all our hearts.
The evening eye shines down on earth
    a prayer for our continued birth.

We lift our hearts in tender praise
and give you thanks for all our days.
—Macrina Wiederkehr

(This song can be found on the CD *Seven Sacred Pauses: Singing Mindfully Dawn Through Dark*.)

Contemporary Psalm

Antiphon: In the evening of life we shall be judged by love. (John of the Cross)

Oh Gracious Giver of the Day,
bountiful has been my daily bread;
and in the heart of sorrows
you have surrounded me with grace.

Like the earth circling the sun,
blessings have circled my day.
As the lamps of evening are lit,
I live in the circling.

My eyes scan the horizons
of your goodness.
Standing tall with thanksgiving
I praise you with a grateful heart.

O Mystery within Mystery,
touch the paradoxes of this day
with your healing breath.

Let your mantle of peace
clothe me in this evening hour.
It is well with my soul.
All shall be well; all shall be well.

—Macrina Wiederkehr

Repeat Antiphon.

Biblical Psalm Suggestions for the Twilight Hour

Psalm 34
Psalm 139
Psalm 145

Closing Prayer

Select the Prayer of the Hour below or another prayer in this section.

Prayer of the Hour

Stay with Us, Lord, for the Day Is Almost Over . . .

Come, sit at our table. Be present in the bread we break and share. It is our daily bread lifted out of both grace and struggle. It is the bread of compassion and joy, sorrow and courage. We bless you who have journeyed with us through the hours of this day. Now it is evening, and the day is almost spent. Come to our supper table. Be our guest. Let us see your face in each of our table companions. At this Vespers hour light the lamps of our hearts and attend our deepest hungers. May it be so!

Additional Prayers and Poems for the Twilight Hour

O You Whose Face Is a Thousand Colors . . .

Look upon us in this twilight hour, and color our faces with the radiance of your love. As the light of the sun fades away, light the lamps of our hearts that we may see one another more clearly. Let the incense of our gratitude rise as our hearts become full of music and song. May the work that we bring with us into this hour fall away from our minds as we enter into the mystical grace of the evening hour. Amen.

O Twilight Face of God . . .

As I take off my work clothes I put on a robe of gratitude. Thank you for all the blessings of this day, even those I have not yet recognized. Look kindly on the household in which I live. Teach me to relax and hand over the day. I long to be part of the joy of this evening hour. The lamps of evening have been lit. Let me be your shining as the day fades away. In Christ's name we pray.

Meditation on the thin places of your day . . .

In this evening hour reflect on the thin places of your day. Recall those moments when you stood very near the glory of God. There may be more than you realize. That's why it's important to take time for solitude. Practice deep listening and deep breathing. After a few moments of silence, the prayer below may help you bring closure to your day.

O Spirit of the Holy One, earth is turning from the sun. Day is almost done. Radiant face of the Divine, clothe me now for the evening hour. As I stand before the thin places, lift the veil that hides your presence. Show me your face O God. Robe me in twilight. I am a companion of day and night. One hand cradles the daylight; the other embraces night. I have come to the Vespers hour. Day is almost done.

Let Evening Come Upon Us

Let evening come upon us
and bring your peace, O Lord.
Let hearts be stilled in quiet
and listen to your Word.

Let day sink into nighttime
and darkness close around.
We lift our hearts to praise you,
to seek and to be found.

Let us be gathered into one
and inner turmoil end.

Lord, calm our restless spirits now,
let gentle rest descend.

—Judith Brower, O.S.B.

The Twilight Hour

Twilight is the poet's hour,
twilight is the soul's deep love.
Light from heaven, accessible,
light and darkness become one.

As the curtain of day falls away,
the curtain of night is rising.
In the falling and the rising
the star of God's face shines forth.

O blessed, holy twilight,
heaven's face unveiled.
soft glow of sundown
night glow through sunray.

This is the mystical hour,
day fading; night rising.
Sweet space between day and night,
ask what you will and it shall be done.
This is the hour of grace.

—Macrina Wiederkehr

Praying the Sunset Prayer

I'll let you in on a secret
about how one should pray
the sunset prayer.
It's a juicy bit of praying,
like strolling on grass,
nobody's chasing you,
nobody hurries you.
You walk toward your Creator
with gifts in pure, empty hands.
The words are golden,
their meaning is transparent,
it's as though you're saying them
for the first time.

If you don't catch on
that you should feel a little elevated,
you're not saying the sunset prayer.
The tune is sheer simplicity,
you're just lending a helping hand
to the sinking day.
It's a heavy responsibility.
You take a created day
and you slip it
into the archive of life,
where all our lived-out days
are lying together.

The day is departing with a quiet kiss.
It lies open at your feet

while you stand saying the blessings.
You can't create anything yourself,
but you can lead the day to its end
and see clearly the smile
of its going down.

See how whole it is,
not diminished for a second,
how you age with the days
that keep dawning,
how you bring your lived-out day
as a gift to eternity.

—Jacob Glatstein

Antiphons for the Twilight Hour

In the evening of life I shall be judged by love.
—John of the Cross

To, thee, whose temple is all space,
whose altar, earth, sea, skies,
one chorus let all being raise;
all nature's incense rise!

—Alexander Pope

The touch of an Eternal Presence thrills
the fringes of the sunsets and the hills.

—Richard Realf

By day the Lord commands his steadfast love,
and at night his song is with me,
a prayer to the God of my life.

—Psalm 42:8

O send out your light and your truth; let them lead me;
let them bring me to your holy hill and to your dwelling.

—Psalm 43:3

Beauty is life when life unveils her holy face.
But you are the life and you are the veil.

—Kahlil Gibran

In the twilight of life, God will not judge us on our earthly
possessions and human success, but rather on how much we
have loved.

—John of the Cross

And we are put on earth, a little space, that we learn to bear
the beams of love.

—William Blake

There have been evenings when the light has turned everything silver, and like you I have stopped at a corner and suddenly staggered with the grace of it all.

—William Stafford

The hours are appointed and named; they are the Lord's.
Life's fretfulness is transcended. The different and the novel
are sweet, but regularity and repetition are also teachers.

—Mary Oliver

Just as plants die and are reborn, we too each day lay to rest
what we did that day and awake to a new sunrise.

—Dorothy Stang, S.N.D. de N.

A desire to kneel down sometimes pulses through my body,
or rather it is as if my body had been meant and made for
the act of kneeling. Sometimes in moments of deep gratitude,
kneeling down becomes an overwhelming urge, head deeply
bowed, hand before my face.

—Etty Hillesum

O Lord, support us all the day long, until the shadows
lengthen, and the evening comes, and the busy world is
hushed, and the fever of life is over, and our work is done.
Then, Lord, in your mercy grant us a safe lodging, and a holy
rest, and peace at the last; through Jesus Christ our Lord.

—John Henry Newman

A soul flare is what happens when someone shines [his or her]
light no matter what it is. In a song, a smile, or a well-made
soup; they send out a flare of light that inspires others to
shine their own. Soul flares make this world better.

—Annie O'Shaughnessy

seven

the great silence

Themes for the hour:
silence, rest, and sleep
darkness, trust, and protection
personal sorrow, completion, intimacy

Night

Stars pierce the darkness of the night sky. The holiness of night enfolds me. Angels of protection surround me. As I enter the Great Silence, I thoughtfully attend to my heart. With eyes of mercy and delight I scan my actions of this day. Are the achievements of this day aligned with my heart's deepest yearning for grace-filled living? Gratitude and compassion rise up from my soul like incense: gratitude for the blessings of the day, compassion for the discouragements of the day. I prayerfully hold in my heart the ones who have passed through my life this day. Silence and darkness fall upon me like a great protective quilt of love. Under the careful guidance of the angels and the Queen of Heaven, I put away my fear of the night and my reluctance to enter the silence. Like a bird going home to roost at the end of the day I, too, seek my rest. I enter the comforting darkness, robed in trust and confident of divine protection. The deep silence of the hour blesses me; the sweet darkness anoints me. The living prayer of this day, now complete, I offer to the Beloved.

You are my lamp, O God,
you brighten the darkness around me.
—2 Samuel 22:29

From the twilight path of Vespers with its mystical shadows and its wake of color, we move now into the shades of night. We move into the Great Silence. Our night prayer, Compline, is the completion of our journey through the seasons of the day. The word *compline* comes from the same Latin root as the word *complete.* The mood of Compline is more subjective than the other hours. We look within more than without. This is a personal prayer for one who wants to make peace with God, community, and self before retiring for the night. Repentance and personal sorrow for sin are among the themes for this hour.

Silence and darkness are two important images offered for our night prayer. We have lived this day as well as we were able. We come now to the moment when there is nothing more to see or hear, nothing more to say. Silence is for the ears as darkness is for the eyes. We travel within to the deep places where we do not need words or images. This mystical place is difficult for most modern-day people. Pre-industrial people were more comfortable in this place of darkness and silence. It is true they were not living in an advanced technological society, yet every age has its gift to offer the universe. As we grow away from the age of silence and darkness, we may need to ask ourselves if this "growing away from" is partially responsible for a loss of soul in today's world. When I go into households in which every room has a TV blaring, often with no one listening, I sense acutely that something is absent in many people's daily lives and they don't even notice the absence. At times like this I want to suggest that we look back to the ancestors to see if there might be a lost gift waiting to be found.

A friend describes the sickness that is sweeping through our land in this way: It's common to rush through dinner with the kids, help them with homework, put them to bed and get organized for the next school day. At 10 p.m. she may be sitting in bed with the TV on to check the next day's weather while reading the mail, paying bills, and checking e-mail.

Perhaps my friend is right, and our cultural poverty is indeed our ignorance of the value of silence, mindfulness, conscious reflection, rest, and sleep. Monastic communities have tried to keep alive that mystic place within where it is possible to live without noise, images, or words. Compline is the hour that calls us back to the natural rhythms of light and darkness, rest and wakefulness.

Compline begins with an invitation to be vigilant and strong in faith. We are to be ever watchful so that the enemies of the soul will not find us careless and unaware. Listening to this plea for vigilance, we apply it to our personal lives. The enemies of the soul are all around us. Who among us is not acquainted with these undesired guests that visit us on a daily basis: apathy, indifference, self-righteousness, greed, control, selfishness, lust, resentments, bitterness. . . . Only you can finish the list. The obstacles to spiritual and human development are plentiful. Most of us are quite familiar with those things that detain us on our day's journey. Assistance for our spiritual and human growth is also available. As we become more faithful in pausing for reflection, these spiritual resources will reveal themselves to us.

We are encouraged to begin our night prayer with a simple "consciousness examen." This is a form of prayer that makes it possible for us to be aware of and learn from the experiences of our day. To assist you in processing this I have included a short examen in the Prayer Guide that comes after this reflection. I prefer the term consciousness examen rather than examination of conscience. Putting the focus on the word *examination* can suggest a probing kind of insensitive analysis. Using the word *consciousness* as our focal point, we are drawn into a more gentle way of evaluating our day. The focus is on awareness, and we include not just the weaknesses and unconscious moments of our day but also the strengths and accomplishments.

The symbol of light has been a companion on our journey through the hours. Light is a strong scriptural and liturgical image used often in prayer. When we pause at midday it is obvious that this is the hour of radiance. However, we have journeyed through a number of hours since midday. The shadows have lengthened, and we are no longer dwelling in the land of light. The shadow of darkness is upon us.

Just as the church uses the image of light to help us become conscious of the holiness of our lives, so too themes of darkness are used to remind us that some forms of darkness have the power to hide the light of our goodness. Darkness is often associated with sin. Many of us fear the darkness. We fear what we cannot see. When too much darkness surrounds us, we seek protection. Protection is one of the themes of this hour. We ask to be protected from unhealthy kinds of darkness. We pray to be sheltered under the shadow of God's wings.

There are various kinds of darkness. I would like to address first sin and suffering.

The darkness of sin is familiar terrain. In regard to sin I sometimes think we suffer from two heresies. The old heresy is that everything is a sin, and the new heresy is that nothing is a sin. Perhaps we need to look carefully at the meaning of sin. It is part of the human condition, and no matter what name we give it, sin is an obstacle that prevents us from being our best selves. It hides the truth from us and causes us to forget that we are individuals created in the divine image. We all have unwanted obstacles in our lives. We need to learn how to be healthy sinners, living neither in denial regarding our sin nor in despair because of sin. Rather, we live in the light of God's compassion. We are loved sinners.

Another kind of darkness is the suffering that is so much a part of every life. Some of the suffering is because of the effects of sin. So much of the violence from which all of creation suffers comes from greed and misuse of power. When we choose to live in ignorance and prejudice, we choose to remain in darkness. From this kind of darkness we need protection and healing. There is also the suffering of sickness and death that leaves gaping holes of grief in our souls. This form of darkness can end up working for our good because it teaches us lessons of vulnerability and trust. We learn to put our faith in God and in those who care for us. In our night prayer, then, we pray for protection as we remember the darkness all over the world and the many places where our sisters and brothers may be in danger of harmful confrontations, violence, wrong choices, and suffering. We behold the guardian of the night, ever present in our midst to protect us from danger. As we try to enter deeply into the pain of the world, our sorrow becomes a cosmic sorrow as well as personal sorrow.

Although darkness has often been associated with fear and evil, I would like to offer yet another face of darkness for our night prayer. This darkness is not one we need protection from, but rather is a darkness we are invited to enter. It is a bit like standing before the hidden face of the divine, longing for entrance yet fully aware that we know so little about the one we call God. The poet Lee Self beautifully addresses this haunting desire for entrance into the Eternal Mystery. In her poem "Incorrigible Exuberance Shared," she describes well the incurable delight that draws us into the Holy Darkness of God.

> What I know of You is meager.
> What I love of You is intense.
> What spills from me because of You is beyond
>   measure.
>
> You bait me with Your nothing that is everything
>   to me.
> You lead me on with promises that I must depend
>   on You to fulfill.
> You teach me with sorrow, joy, peace, and anger,
>   with anything I can muster.
>
> You are extravagant with your love.
> You drown me with devotion and understanding.
> You leave me breathless, thoughtless.

Master, Teacher, Friend, Lover, Parent, Creator,
  Redeemer, Sustainer . . .

I try to encompass all your names but they slip
  from my grasp.
When I hold nothing, I hold You.
When I hold you, I hold everything.

—Lee Self

Truly there is an incurable delight drawing us into the
Holy Darkness of God. In the heart of this darkness we learn
silence and surrender, for there is nothing we need to say.
One of these faces of darkness is intimacy with the Beloved.
In both human and divine love we experience darkness as
a pathway for intimacy. The writings of John of the Cross
clearly give witness to the beauty of darkness and spiritual
intimacy with the Beloved.

One dark night
fired by love's urgent longing
ah, the sheer grace—
I went out unseen,
my house being now all stilled
. . . with no other light or guide
than the one that burned in my heart.

—John of the Cross

The darkness can be exquisitely beautiful and restful. In
the darkness we can view the stars. Seeds need darkness for
gestation and growth. The baby grows in the darkness of the
womb. Too much light can be blinding. There is a softness
in darkness.

There are times when the darkness of suffering opens up whole new vistas of growth and insight in our lives that, perhaps, we could never have learned in the light. Helen Keller describes her faith, in the midst of permanent silence and darkness, as a "spiritual strong searchlight." Her remarkable words can serve as a portion of your meditation for this night hour.

> Observers in the full enjoyment of their bodily senses pity me, but it is because they do not see the golden chamber in my life where I dwell delighted; for, dark as my path may seem to them, I carry a magic light in my heart. Faith, the spiritual strong searchlight, illumines the way, and although sinister doubts lurk in the shadow, I walk unafraid toward the enchanted wood where the foliage is always green, where joy abides, where nightingales nest and sing, and where life and death are one in the Presence of the Lord.

As I read these words, I am deeply moved by the positive tone of this message coming from one who was engulfed in a lifetime of darkness and silence. Such an attitude seems little less than miraculous. And yet, we all have within us a magic light. It is the "holy lamp inside my heart" that Hafiz referred to (c.f. The Awakening Hour). The prophet Samuel also acknowledged it when he said, "You are my lamp, O Lord" (2 Sm 22:29). And it is the light Jesus was speaking of when he told us, "You are the light of the world" (Mt 5:14). It is the "sanctifying grace" that Catholics believe is a share in God's very own life. When shadows fall and darkness seems too deep for comfort, we need the faith that Helen Keller speaks of—the faith she calls her *spiritual strong searchlight*. We need to practice seeing in the dark. We need to remember to use our magic light of love, the light within.

At a very tender age I was aware of that magic light. I have vivid memories of dancing with the light and the dark as a young child. I would go out of our farmhouse into the big dark yard; I would go far enough away from the house so that I could enjoy the beauty of the starry night sky all alone. I was not totally fearless about being alone in the dark. There were no street lights out in the country, so it was truly dark. I tolerated my fear because I loved the stars so much. There was a bit of unease lurking in my heart, and so I would keep looking back at our house where I could see the light shining through the windows. My eyes would glance toward the night sky and the faraway lights—then back to the farm house with its comforting closer-to-home lights. It was a bit like a dance with the faraway lights and the close-to-home lights. The heavens were filled with mystery; home was filled with safety and love. The heavens were full of the unknown; home was surrounded with the known. Then suddenly my apprehension would win out and I would rush back to the comfort of the close-to-home lights. I love that memory, and as I recall it now, it has a semblance of the dance between the transcendent and imminent God.

There is something of the darkness we do not feel and know experientially in the bright lights of the city. The poet Baron Wormser eloquently describes the unique experience of truly receiving the darkness. Listen to his marvelous description of the slow and soft descent of darkness:

The first evening after we moved into our house in the woods, it started to get dark, and I thought, It is getting dark. That seems simple-minded, but what I felt was vividly complex. Night's coming was so profound, so transfixing, so soft yet indelible that I was startled and lulled in the same awed moment. I remember very clearly feeling how, second by tiny second, the dark was creeping in, how night "fell"—a great, slow curtain—how darkness "grew"—something organic yet rooted in the ineffable. Poets have written endlessly about the melancholy and charm of dusk, the time of haunting regret. I could feel that mood as I watched the waning light. It was fluid, like ink in water. There was no switch to hit to banish the dark, to join the bright ranks of the electrified world.

The hour of Compline, conclusion of the day, opens a window to the night. We are invited to walk the path of darkness and silence. Early monastic communities, most likely, prayed Compline in the dark, thus the symbol of entering the darkness and praying for protection was especially potent. The content of Compline, being always the same, was easy to memorize. Although today we have some flexibility in designing our night prayer, there will always be a piece of my heart that leans toward this ancient beauty of our traditional Compline.

Historically, night prayer closes with a hymn to Mary. In some communities the lights are dimmed or turned out and the closing hymn is sung in the darkness. Mary knew much about waiting in silence and darkness. We can only imagine her moments of waiting: waiting for the birth of her son, for the mystery enshrouded in his growing up, the meaning of his teachings; waiting at the foot of the cross and at the tomb; waiting for the Spirit. This faithful woman, the mother of Jesus, lived through many of the same holy darkness prayers that we live through each day.

Although St. Benedict did not include the Canticle of Simeon as part of Compline, this beautiful canticle is often prayed during night prayer. It offers us the lovely image of Mary and Joseph offering Jesus in the temple. Simeon, who is old in age and wisdom, has waited all his life for this moment. With joy he takes the child in his arms and sings his famous swan song:

> Now you can dismiss your servant in peace.
> Your word has become flesh in my sight.
> My eyes have beheld the One I kept vigil for all
>   my life.
> Here is your saving grace raised high for all to see.
> Here is the wonder of your revelation, the glory of
>   your people.
>
> —Luke 2:29–32 (paraphrased)

These words belong to us all. Has Christ not been presented to us in a thousand faces? Is it not true that in our own era we, too, are asked to be light for the people with whom we dwell? Are we not called to be God's glory for those in our midst? Simeon's canticle can become our swan song also. Day is done, and we have accomplished what was possible for us to accomplish this day. We have kept vigil through the hours of light, faithful to the invitation of the moments. Now it is time to let go of the day.

Of course what Simeon is really saying is, "I am ready to die." For monastics, sleep is seen as a little death, and so it can be a preparation for the larger death. The beginning prayer for Compline is: May almighty God grant us a peaceful night and a happy death. Our night prayer helps us prepare for death: the daily dyings and the final physical death. Compline is the quiet night prayer of trust in which we place ourselves in divine hands.

Compline always ends with what monastics call the "great silence." We move into the healing silence of the night where we can rest from the day's labors. Silence is like a river of grace inviting us to leap unafraid into its beckoning depths. It is dark and mysterious in the waters of grace. Yet in the silent darkness we are given new eyes. In the heart of the divine we can see more clearly who we are. We are renewed and cleansed in this river of silence. There are those among you who fear the Great Silence. It is a foreign land to you. Sometimes it is good to leap into the unknown. Practice leaping. Practice surrendering. God will hold you. Silence will teach you.

As we fall into the deep, dark silence of the night, we invite God's protective angels to dwell in our houses and our hearts—all the angels: guardian angels, the great angels who are messengers of good news and healing and strength, the angel who wrestled through the night with Jacob and gave him a new name. Surround yourself with angels all through the night. Perhaps you, too, will awaken with a new name.

Prayers, Poetry, and Antiphons to Help You Celebrate the Great Silence

A Prayer Guide

Opening

O Holy One, in whose light and shadows we have journeyed through this day,
• give us now a peaceful night and when our lives have ripened, a happy death!

Examen

Let us be watchful and vigilant because the enemies of the soul prowl about looking for opportune moments to discourage us. Remember then, with confidence, the powerful and strong spiritual searchlight of faith and the magic light within. Let us place ourselves in the protective care of the angels and into the cupped hands of the Divine.

Take a moment to let these images embrace you. Use the following Examen of Consciousness as a careful reflection of your day, or create your own:

- Have I been a good memory in anyone's life today?
- Have the ears of my heart opened to the voice of God?
- Have the ears of my heart opened to the needs of my sisters and brothers?
- Have the eyes of my heart beheld the Divine face in all created things?
- What do I know, but live as though I do not know?
- Have I been a good student of the hours today?
- How have I affected the quality of this day?
- Have I been blind or deaf to the blessings of the day?
- Is there anyone, including myself, whom I need to forgive?
- When did I experience my heart opening wide today?
- Have I worked with joy or drudgery?
- Have I waited with grace or with impatience?
- What is the one thing in my life that is standing on tip-toe crying, "May I have your attention please?" What needs my attention?

Contemporary Psalm

Antiphon: I yearn to be held in the great hands of your heart—oh let them take me now.

Into them I place these fragments, my life, and
you, God—spend them however you want. (Rainer
Maria Rilke)

O Caregiver of the Night,
Sweet Soul of the Darkness,
send angels to protect and anoint me,
protect me from darkness that can harm,
anoint me with darkness that can bless.

In this hour of deep silence
when all things are hushed,
I carve out a space in the darkness
for you, O Beloved, to dwell.
In the quiet of the night I seek your face.
Shine upon me and I shall be healed.

Pour out the blessing of your presence on all
who retire to their beds in sorrow and fear.
Comfort those who have no silence.
Shelter those who have no peace.
Surprise them with your love.

Summon me into your beautiful darkness.
Lead me to the land of rest.
Cherish my every breath while sleeping
and I will rise at dawn
with the memory of you in my heart.

Repeat Antiphon.

Biblical Psalm Suggestions for the Great Silence

Psalm 23
Psalm 91
Psalm 134

Closing Prayer

Select the Prayer of the Hour below or another prayer in this section.

Prayer of the Hour

O Gracious Lover of Our Souls . . .

Let your comforting darkness embrace us this night. The beautiful prayer of this day is complete. This day's pilgrimage is ending, and we hold dear the lessons of the hours. Night has fallen. Breathe us into this good night. Calm our hearts. Comfort our souls. Protect us from danger. Fill us with well-being. Anoint us with your loving protection. Receive our prayer. Amen. Amen.

With candles lit, sit in the darkness. Listen to this haunting song from Velma Frye's CD, Seven Sacred Pauses: Singing Mindfully Dawn Through Dark.

O Beautiful Darkness,

> The arms of darkness hold us,
> revealing now how dear we are.
> O Beautiful Darkness. O Comforting Darkness.
>
> Enfold us and hold us.
> Inform us, transform us.
> O Beautiful Darkness. O Comforting Darkness.
>
> Surround us, all around us,
> and hold our light like sky to star.
> O Beautiful Darkness. O Comforting Darkness.
> —Macrina Wiederkehr

Additional Prayers and Poems for the Great Silence

O You Who Began It All . . .

I am listening to the night. Everything is singing. Do you hear the little things with wings that fly through the air and live in trees and meadows? Everything is humming the song of night. Do you hear your forest creatures and their night songs? And we, your beloved creatures who can only fly in our imaginations, we, too, fly with joy to the refuge of your heart, singing our night songs. We sing to end the day. Each heart has a deep throat that longs to pour forth melodies. O

Divine Song Catcher, receive our songs of silent praise. Lay your hand upon our souls and give us rest.

Dancer of the Distant Stars . . .

Now the day is over. Gently dance us out of this day into the arms of night. Give us peaceful rest. Night, with all its beauty, is falling upon us. Let the star dust of your love descend on us throughout this night. O Mysterious Beauty, you are an ancient melody in our lives. Your music lingers in our souls, lulling us to sleep peacefully in the shadow of your wings. O Dancer of the Distant Stars, we are part of your starlight. Renew us and restore us as we sleep. May all your creatures have a Good Night.

Visit O Lord . . .

This dwelling place and drive far away all snares of the enemy. May your holy angels dwell among us and keep us in peace, and let your blessing be always upon us.

—Monastic Breviary

A Hymn to Mary

Queen of the heavens, we greet you,
gracious Lady of all the angels;
you are dawn and door of morning,
whence the world's true light is risen.

Joy to you, O maiden glorious,
beautiful beyond all others.
Honor to you, O most gracious.
Intercede for us always to Jesus.

—Anonymous, twelfth century

Night Rain

Burrowed deep in my bed
I hear the rain fall
weightily in the garden,
sweep the roof with galloping gusts,
indifferent to my plights.

I fall asleep with poems
dropping from the sky,
caught beyond my eyelids
by nocturnal leafy arms.

All night long they murmur.
In the morning I awake
with poetry on my lips.

—Antoinette Voûte Roeder

Antiphons for the Great Silence

You are my lamp, O Lord!
O my God, You brighten the darkness about me.

—2 Samuel 22:29 (NAB)

As soon as I lie down I fall peacefully asleep,
for you alone, O Lord, bring security to my dwelling.
—Psalm 4:9 (NAB)

I yearn to be held in the great hands of your heart—oh let
them take me now. Into them I place these fragments, my
life, and you, God—spend them however you want.
—Rainer Maria Rilke

Look at the stars! look, look up at the skies!
O look at all the fire-folk sitting in the air!
—Gerard Manley Hopkins

And if tonight my soul may find her peace, and sink in good
oblivion,
and in the morning wake like a new-opened flower
then I have been dipped again in God, and new-created.
—D.H. Lawrence

I saw eternity the other night
like a great ring of pure and endless light.
—Henry Vaughn

Protect us, Lord, as we stay awake; watch over us as we
sleep,
that awake, we may keep watch with Christ,
and asleep, rest in his peace.
—The Liturgy of the Hours

Too late have I loved you, oh Beauty so ancient yet ever new!
Too late have I loved you! And behold, you were within me
and I out of myself, and there I searched for you.

—St. Augustine

The more faithfully you listen to the voice within you, the
better you hear what is sounding outside of you.

—Dag Hammarskjöld

Night holds no terrors for me sleeping under God's wings.

—The Liturgy of the Hours

Stillness is what creates Love.
Movement is what creates Life.
To be still, yet still moving, that is everything.

—Do Hyun Choe

Only in silence the word, only in dark the light,
only in dying life.

—Ursula K. Le Guin

By day the Lord commands his steadfast love; and at night his
song is with me, a prayer to the God of my life.

—Psalm 42:8

O Most High, when I am afraid, I put my trust in you.

—Psalm 56:3

Finish each day and be done with it. You have done what you could. Some blunders and absurdities have crept in; forget them as soon as you can. Tomorrow is a new day.

—Ralph Waldo Emerson

When I stand before God at the end of my life, I would hope that I would not have a single bit of talent left and could say, "I used everything you gave me."

—Erma Bombeck

There comes a moment when attention must be paid. . . . A time to embrace mystery as my native land. And silence as my native tongue.

—John Kirvan

Litany of the Hours

Dear Artist of the Universe, Beloved Sculptor, Singer, and Author of my life, born of your image I have made a home in the open fields of your heart. The magnetic tug of your invitation to grow is slowly transforming me into a gift for the world. Mentor me into healthy ways of living.

—Help me remember to pause.

Make of me a faithful vigil in the heart of darkness, I want to be a sentinel through all the dark hours. When the deep darkness falls, let me be your star. Name me One Who Watches Through the Night. Reveal to me the holiness of lingering with mystery. Employ me in the holy art of waiting.

—O teach me to live with a vigilant heart.

Make of me a dawn. Let me be a small voice of joy, rising with the sun. Color me with sunrise. Let me be your awakening first light of new day. Make me a joyful, unexpected surprise in the lives of many, an everlasting birthday. I want to be your goodness rising, your grace poured forth in every hour. Name me Dawn, sweet beginning of every day, gift for a sleepy world.

—O make of me a rising dawn.

Make of me a midmorning blessing. As you breathe me into this day, let me become your breath. Transform me into early morning sun, bright with potential and possibility. Let me be your love made visible. Sing through me in the midmorning hours. Make me your musical instrument.

—Strum a melody of blessing with my life.

Make me your noonday sun, bright with passion, on fire with truth, enduringly courageous. Let me be light for the world. Create in me a nonviolent heart. O let me be your heart. Help me believe the truth about myself no matter how beautiful it is. Let me be the peace for which I pray. Teach me to energize others, to stir up their enthusiasm without overwhelming them.

—Make my power to love stronger than my love of power.

Make of me a midafternoon shadow that I may soften the intensity of the sun. Let me be shade. Robe me with wisdom. Enable me to be at home with impermanence. Teach me the dance of surrender. O make of me a great letting go. May the sacred emptiness of my life help others to know fullness. May I never fear a death that brings me life.

—Let me rejoice in the harvest of each dying day.

Make of me a twilight: wake of color, trail of glory. In the evening of life transform me into a song of gratitude. I want to be an evening star for those who have lost their way. I want to be beauty at the end of each day. On my pilgrimage through the day, write mystery stories with my life. Out of my faithful attendance to the hours pour forth the incense of your praise.

—Transform me into a song of gratitude.

Make me your holy darkness, your blessed night. Transform me into a great silence that drowns out distracting noises. Fashion me into one who sees with the eyes of the soul. I long to be a protective mantle of comforting darkness for all who need rest. Give me insight into the Holy Mystery that cradles me through the night.

—O make of me your night prayer.

O Eternal Now,

Help me remember to pause on my daily pilgrimage through the hours. Teach me to live with a vigilant heart. Make of me a rising dawn. Strum a melody of blessing with my life. Make my power to love stronger than my love of power. Let me rejoice in the harvest of each dying day. Transform me into a song of gratitude. Make of me your night prayer. Enfold me in the circle of your Time-Enduring-Now, even as it was in the beginning and shall be forever. Amen.

—Macrina Wiederkehr

Chants

The lyrics that follow are taken from *Seven Sacred Pauses: Singing Mindfully Dawn Through Dark* by Velma Frye. Some of these chants correspond to the Sacred Song in the Prayer Guide for each hour. Others may be selected as additional songs for the various hours. The CD is available from www. velmafrye.com.

Velma Frye is a composer, recording artist, and performer, most notably on Garrison Keillor's *A Prairie Home Companion*. With two degrees in music from Florida State University, she also teaches piano, leads singing circles, and writes about music education. She lives in Tallahassee, Florida, and is married with two children.

The Night Watch

1. The Angel of Night
(Macrina Wiederkehr, Velma Frye)

The angel of night lights a candle in my soul.
The angel of night lights a candle in my soul.
And summoned from sleep I am drawn to the
    One,
To the One who waits for me.
For deep listening, deep waiting, deep watching
    now.
The angel of night lights a candle in my soul.
The angel of night lights a candle in my soul.
For deep listening, deep waiting, deep watching
    now
With the One who waits for me.

2. Sacred Darkness
(Macrina Wiederkehr, Velma Frye)

In this sacred darkness I sit in silence.
Open in this moment, I trust in the darkness.
Waiting in trust, growing in trust,
Waiting and trusting the sacred darkness.
I surrender.
I surrender.
I surrender.

3. Keeping Vigil with the Mystery
(Macrina Wiederkehr, Velma Frye)

> My heart can see into the darkness.
> And my prayer travels deep, where the Eternal One
>   waits.
> With love I listen, keeping vigil with the Mystery,
> With the One who waits for me.
> I am with the One who waits for me.

The Awakening Hour

4. O Living Breath of God
(Macrina Wiederkehr, Velma Frye)

> O living breath of God awaken us this day.
> O living breath of God awaken us this day.
> Open the windows of our souls.
> Open the walls of our minds.
> Open the doors of our hearts.
> Awaken us to hope. Awaken us to joy.
> Awaken us to the coming of the light.

5. Being Awake
(Macrina Wiederkehr, Velma Frye)

> Set the clock of your heart.
> Set the clock of your heart.
>
> Breathe in the dawn.
> Breathe in the dawn.
>
> Raise high the chalice of your life.
> Taste the joy, the joy of being awake!
>
> It's the best medicine of all.
> Being awake! Being awake!
>
> Set the clock of your heart, awake!
> Breathe, being awake!
>
> Taste the joy, the joy of being awake!
> Being awake! Being awake!

6. Morning Light
(Macrina Wiederkehr, Velma Frye)

> Rising from the night, we reach for morning rays.
> We bathe ourselves in shining light, and clothe
>   ourselves with day.
>
> Morning light help us find peace of mind this day.
> Morning light help us find peace of mind this day.
>
> Holding cradled hands, we lift our empty bowls.
> The light of dawn fills to the brim our hungry,
>   weary souls.

Morning light help us find peace of mind this day.
Morning light help us find peace of mind this day.

The Blessing Hour

7. Blessings of the Morning
(Velma Frye)

Blessings. Blessings.
Blessings as the day unfolds, blessings of the
     morning,
Pausing in the fullness of the moment, our grateful
     hearts

Sing a morning song on this holy ground.
Sing a morning song to precious life all around.

Blessings. Blessings.
Blessings of the rising sun, blessings of the
     morning,
Pausing in the fullness of the moment, our grateful
     hearts

Sing a morning song on this holy ground.
Sing a morning song to precious life all around.
Blessings. Blessings. Blessings of the morning.

8. What Is
(Macrina Wiederkehr and Velma Frye, with thanks to
Emily Dickinson for "I dwell in possibility")

I stand before what is with an open heart.
And with an open heart I dwell in possibility.
And now I stand before what is with an open
    heart.

9. Spirit of the Morning
(Macrina Wiederkehr, Velma Frye)

Spirit of the morning, breathe into my temple.
Spirit of the morning, breathe into my temple.
Refresh my mind. Renew my heart.
Spirit of the morning. O spirit of the morning.

Spirit of the morning, bless this work I have
    begun.
Spirit of the morning, bless this work I have
    begun.
Give me courage! Give me strength!
Spirit of the morning. O spirit of the morning.

The Hour of Illumination

10. Be the Peace
(Macrina Wiederkehr, Velma Frye)

In this the hour of the noonday sun,
We raise our hands to the peaceful one.
And now is the hour to pray for peace,
For kindness, compassion to increase.

So let us be the change we wish to see.
Let us bow to each other and say
That we will be the peace for which we long.
This is our promise. This is our song.

Before we share the noon-day meal,
Our deepest hungers let us feel.
May all be fed. May all be well.
May all of God's children in the garden dwell.
So let us be the change we wish to see.
Let us bow to each other and say
That we will be the peace for which we long.
This is our promise. This is our song.

Now is the hour for peace to flower.
Now is the hour for peace to flower.
Now is the hour for peace to flower.
Now is the hour for peace to flower.

May all be fed—for peace to flower.
May all be well—for peace to flower.
May all of God's children—for peace to flower,
In the garden dwell—for peace to flower.

Now is the hour!
Now is the hour!
Now is the hour!
Now is the hour!

11. The Truth
(Macrina Wiederkehr, Velma Frye)

I will believe the truth about myself,
no matter how beautiful it is!

12. Dona Nobis Pacem
(anonymous)

Dona nobis pacem, pacem.
Dona nobis pacem.

The Wisdom Hour

13. Let Go and Move
(Candy Butler, Velma Frye)

With all that has been, take lessons, take lessons and
   be grateful.

Let go! Let go! Let go! Let go!
Let go and move! Move on! Move on!

14. Put Everything in Order
(Macrina Wiederkehr, Velma Frye)

Put everything in order as day begins to fade.
Put everything in order as day begins to fade.
All things are passing, moment by moment, breath
    by breath.
All things are passing, moment by moment, birth
    to death.

Take off that cloak of fear. The Divine help you seek
    is here.
And you know you are dying to live. You know you
    are dying to live.

So put everything in order as day begins to fade.
Put everything in order as day begins to fade.

15. I Look into My Heart
(Macrina Wiederkehr, Velma Frye)

I look into my heart for the wisdom, the wisdom,
I look into my heart for the wisdom to live this day
    well.

I look into my heart for the wisdom, the wisdom,
I look into my heart for the wisdom to end this day
    well.

The Twilight Hour

16. Vespers Colors
(Macrina Wiederkehr, Velma Frye)

A thousand colors is your face,
Embracing us with waves of grace.
And as the day-star now departs,
Your glance of light fills all our hearts.
Your glance of light fills all our hearts.

The evening eye shines down on earth,
A prayer for our continued birth.
We lift our hearts in tender praise,
And give you thanks for all our days.
And give you thanks for all our days.

17. Light the Lamps
(Macrina Wiederkehr, Velma Frye)

Light is fading from the sun.
Light of day is almost done.
Spirit of the Holy One,
Clothe us now in twilight,
As we light the lamps of evening.

Earth is turning from the sun.
Light and darkness become one.
Spirit of the Holy One,

Robe us now in twilight,
As we light the lamps of evening.

The curtain of day is falling away,
And the curtain of night is rising.
And in the falling and in the rising
Comes the star of wonder, shining.

Sweet the hour of sweet grace,
As we stand in mystic space.
Spirit of the Holy One,
Clothe us now in twilight,
As we light the lamps of evening.

18. Day Is Done
(Traditional, new words: Velma Frye)

Day is done. Gone the sun, from the lake, from the
    hills, from the sky.
All is well. Safely rest, you and I. You and I.

Thanks and praise for our days, for our nights 'neath
    the moon, 'neath the stars.
As we go, this our prayer: Peace to all, near and far.

The Great Silence

19. O Beautiful Darkness
(Macrina Wiederkehr, Velma Frye)

The arms of darkness hold us,
Revealing now how dear we are.
O beautiful darkness. O comforting darkness.
O beautiful darkness. O comforting darkness.

Enfold us and hold us.
Inform us, transform us.
O beautiful darkness. O comforting darkness.
O beautiful darkness. O comforting darkness.

Surround us, all around us,
And hold our light, like sky to star.
O beautiful darkness. O comforting darkness.
O beautiful darkness. O comforting darkness.

20. A Lullaby for After Dark—Be Still
(Macrina Wiederkehr, Velma Frye)

Be still. Be still. Be still. Be still.
Go deep into the silence of the night.
And robe yourself in darkness.
See with the heart into the dark of the night.
So silent the night.
So dark the night.
Be still. Be still.

Be still. Be still.
Be still. Be still.

21. All Through the Night
(Traditional Welsh)

Sleep, my child, and peace attend thee, all through
the night.
Guardian angels Love will send thee, all through the
night.
Soft the drowsy hours are creeping, hill and dale in
slumber sleeping,
I, my constant vigil keeping, all through the night.

While the moon, her watch is keeping, all through
the night.
While the weary world is sleeping, all through the
night.
O'er thy spirit gently stealing, visions of delight
revealing,
Breathes a pure and holy feeling, all through the
night.

Notes

Introduction

Pius Parsch, *The Breviary Explained*. St Louis: Herder, 1952, 1953.

Psalm 37 is from *The Psalter*, translated from the Hebrew by the International Commission on English in the Liturgy. Chicago: Liturgy Training Publications, 1995.

Rilke's image of "God's hands" is found in *Book of Hours: Love Poems to God*, translated by Anita Barrows and Joanna Macy. New York: Riverhead Books, 1996.

Living Mindfully

Bede Griffiths, *The Golden String*. New York: P.J. Kennedy & Sons, 1944.

Thomas Merton, *The Way of Chang Tzu*. New York: New Directions, 1965.

The Night Watch

Marcy Heidish, *A Candle at Midnight*. Notre Dame, IN: Ave Maria Press, 2001.

The Awakening Hour

Coleman Barks and Michael Green, *The Illuminated Prayer*. New York: Ballantine Books, 2000.

John Ciardi's poem "The Heron" is from *I marry you; a sheaf of love Poems*. New Brunswick, NJ: Rutgers UP, 1958.

Dom Helder Camara's prayer is from *A Thousand Reasons for Living*. Philadelphia: Fortress Press, 1981.

"Rise Early" originally appeared in a slightly different form in *The Circle of Life,* Joyce Rupp and Macrina Wiederkehr. Notre Dame, IN: Sorin Books, 2005.

"Keeping Watch" is from *I Heard God Laughing*, translated by Daniel Ladinsky. New York: Penguin, 1996, 2002.

Psalm 90 is from *The Psalter*, cited above.

All quotations by Rabindranath Tagore are from *Show Yourself to My Soul*. Notre Dame, IN: Sorin Books, 2002.

The Blessing Hour

All quotations by Kahlil Gibran are from *The Prophet*. New York: Alfred A. Knopf, 1923, 1972.
This chant can be found on the CD by Velma Frye, *Seven Sacred Pauses: Singing Mindfully Dawn Through Dark*.
David Steindl-Rast and Sharon Lebell, *The Music of Silence*. Berkeley, CA: Seastone Press, Second Edition, 2001.
I am grateful to Beth Fritsch, a retreatant at St. Scholastica, for allowing me to use her previously unpublished poem.

The Hour of Illumination

I am grateful to Karen Ewan, a retreatant at St. Scholastica, for allowing me to use her previously unpublished poem.
Dorothy Stang was a member of the Sisters of Notre Dame de Namur who was murdered in the Amazon region of Brazil on February 12, 2005. She was an outspoken advocate for the poor and the environment and had previously received death threats from loggers and land owners.

The Wisdom Hour

Michael Ventura discusses "the Old One" in his article "Reflections On Turning 52" in the *Austin Chronicle* on May 10, 2002. It can be found at www.alternet.org/story/13105.

Tagore's poem is from *Show Yourself to My Soul*, cited above.

I am grateful to Karen Ewan, a retreatant at St. Scholastica, for allowing me to use her previously unpublished poem.

I am grateful to Beth Fritsch, a retreatant at St. Scholastica, for allowing me to use her previously unpublished poem.

The Twilight Hour

Catherine Olsen's article "The Sunset Was My Reminder" was published in *America,* November 20, 2006.

Patricia A. Lunetta's poem "The Visit" was first published in *Presence*, December 2005.

A thousand colors is your Face . . ." originally appeared as part of "A Sunset Vespers Prayer" in *Seasons of Your Heart.* San Francisco: HarperSanFrancisco, 1991.

I am grateful to Judith Brower, O.S.B., of the Monastery of St. Gertrude's for allowing me to use her previously unpublished poem.

"Praying the Sunset Prayer" is from *Selected Poems* of Jacob Glatstein, translated from the Yiddish by Ruth Whitman. New York: October House, 1972.

Cousineau, Phil. *The Soul Aflame, A Modern Book of Hours.*
     Berkeley, CA: Conari Press, 2000.

Deignan, Kathleen, ed., and Thomas Merton. *A Book of
     Hours.* Notre Dame, IN: Sorin Books, 2007.

Hanh, Thich Nhat. *The Miracle of Mindfulness: A Manual on
     Meditation.* Boston: Beacon Press, 1996.

Kabat-Zin, John. *Wherever You Go, There You Are: Mindful-
     ness Meditation in Everyday Life.* New York: Hyperion,
     1994.

Merill, Nan. *Psalms for Praying: An Invitation to Wholeness.*
     New York: Continuum, 2002.

McDaniel, Jay. *Living from the Center.* St. Louis: The Chalice
     Press, 2000.

McKnight, Scot. *Praying with the Church: Developing a Daily
     Rhythm for Spiritual Formation.* Brewster, MA: Paraclete
     Press, 2006.

Newell, Philip J. *Celtic Benediction: Morning and Evening
     Prayer.* Grand Rapids, MI: Wm. B. Eerdmans Publishing,
     2000.

Norris, Gunilla, and Greta Sibley. *Being Home: Discovering
     the Spiritual in the Every Day.* Mahwah, NJ: Hidden
     Spring, 1991.

Richardson, Jan L. *Sacred Journeys: A Woman's Book of Daily
     Prayer.* Nashville: Upper Room Books, 1996.

Silf, Margaret. *Sacred Spaces: Stations on a Celtic Way.*
     Brewster, MA: Paraclete Press, 2001.

Slater, Jonathan. *Mindful Jewish Living: Compassionate Prac-
     tice,* New York: Aviv Press, 2007.

The Great Silence

Lee Self's poem "Incorrigible Exuberance Shared" was first
published in *Presence*, June 2005.

John of the Cross, *The Collected Works of John of the Cross*,
trans. Kieran Kavanaugh, O.C.D., and Otilio Rodriguez,
O.C.D. Washington: Institute of Carmelite Studies,
1971.

Helen Keller, *Midstream: My Later Life.* New York: Green-
wood Press, 1968.

Baron Wormser's article "Feeling Darkness" was published in
Orion, November/December, 2006.

Antoinette Voûte Roeder's poem is from *Weaving the Wind.*
Berkeley, CA: Apocryphile Press, 2006.

Resources
to help you live mindful

Books

Basset, Frederic W., ed. *Awake My Heart: Psalms* Brewster, MA: Paraclete Press, 1998.

Bell, J. Brent. *Holy Silence: The Gift of Quaker Spir* Brewster, MA: Paraclete Press, 2005.

Benson, Robert. *Daily Prayer: A Simple Plan for Lea Say the Daily Prayer of the Church.* Carolina Broac & Publishing, Inc., 2006 (www.dailyprayerlife.con

Brother Lawrence. *The Practice of the Presence of G Spiritual Maxims.* Reading, England: Spire Books, 2000.

Chittister, Joan. *Listen with the Heart: Sacred Mon Everyday Life.* Lanham, MD: Sheed and Ward, 20

The Community of Jesus. *The Little Book of Hours: with the Community of Jesus.* Brewster, MA: P. Press, 2007.

Steindl-Rast, David, and Sharon Lebell. *The Music of Silence: A Sacred Journey Through the Hours of the Day.* Berkeley, CA: Seastone Press, Second Edition, 2001.

Tickle, Phyllis. *The Divine Hours: Prayers for Summertime, A Manual for Prayer.* New York: Doubleday, 2000.

———. *The Divine Hours: Prayers for Autumn and Wintertime.* New York: Image, 2000.

———. *The Divine Hours: Prayers for Springtime.* New York: Image, 2001.

Music

Frye, Velma. *Seven Sacred Pauses: Singing Mindfully Dawn Through Dark.* Tallahassee, FL: Velma Frye, 2007 (www. velmafrye.com).

Macrina Wiederkehr, O.S.B., is a popular retreat guide and author and makes her home with the monastic community of St. Scholastica in Fort Smith, Arkansas. The Benedictine traditions of deep listening to the word of God, and hospitality toward all of life, form the roots of her writing and retreat ministry. Wiederkehr is the best-selling author of six previous books including *A Tree Full of Angels*, *Seasons of Your Heart*, *The Song of the Seed*, *Gold in Your Memories*, *Behold Your Life*, and *The Circle of Life*, which she co-authored with Joyce Rupp. Visit her online at www.macrina-underthesycamoretree.blogspot.com

AVE

AVE MARIA PRESS

Founded in 1865, Ave Maria Press,
a ministry of the Congregation of
Holy Cross, is a Catholic publishing
company that serves the spiritual and
formative needs of the Church and its
schools, institutions, and ministers;
Christian individuals and families; and
others seeking spiritual nourishment.

For a complete listing of titles from

Ave Maria Press

Sorin Books

Forest of Peace

Christian Classics

visit www.avemariapress.com

AVE MARIA PRESS
Notre Dame, IN
A Ministry of the United States Province of Holy Cross